The Internet
A philosophical inquiry

Gordon Graham

London and New York

First published 1999
by Routledge
11 New Fetter Lane, London EC4P 4EE

Simultaneously published in the USA and Canada
by Routledge
29 West 35th Street, New York, NY 10001

Reprinted 2000, 2001, 2002

Routledge is an imprint of the Taylor & Francis Group

© 1999 Gordon Graham

Typeset in Times by Routledge
Printed and bound in Great Britain by St Edmundsbury Press,
Bury St Edmunds, Suffolk

British Library Cataloguing in Publication Data
A catalogue record for this book is available from the British
Library

Library of Congress Cataloging in Publication Data
Graham, Gordon, 1949 July 15–
    The Internet: a philosophical inquiry/Gordon Graham.
    Includes bibliographical references and index.
    1. Internet (computer network) – Philosophy. I. Title.
    TK5105.875.I57G72   1999   99-22325
    004.67' 8–dc21   CIP

ISBN 0–415–19748–1 (hbk)
ISBN 0–415–19749–X (pbk)

The Internet

'Anyone who wants to prepare for a new world coming should read and digest Graham's insights. If knowledge really is power, then *The Internet: A philosophical inquiry* is a power surge.'

David Batstone, *Business 2.0*

'This is a well-written, wide-ranging and, above all, important book.'

Doug Schuler, Seattle Community Network

'Graham has the rare ability to raise provocative issues in a non-technical way.'

Steve Fuller, University of Durham

What should we think about the digital revolution in information technology? As the Internet becomes ever more widespread and extensively used for entertainment, education, shopping, propaganda, government information and personal exchange how are we to understand its nature and the impact it has on our lives? Should we welcome it or fear it?

The Internet: A philosophical inquiry develops many of the themes Gordon Graham presented in his highly successful radio series, 'The Silicon Society'. Radical innovation, moral anarchy, political democracy, censorship, electronic communities and virtual reality are discussed in a clear and stimulating manner with often startling revelations about the wider implications of this technological explosion.

This is an original and fascinating study which subjects the greatest technical advance of today to rigorous philosophical scrutiny, taking us to the heart of questions that none of us can afford to ignore.

Gordon Graham is Regius Professor of Moral Philosophy at the University of Aberdeen and Director of the Aberdeen Centre for Philosophy, Technology and Society. He is also the author of *Philosophy of the Arts* (Routledge, 1997) and *The Shape of the Past* (Oxford University Press, 1997).

For
Lindsay,
who took to computers,
and Murray,
who didn't
– at first

Contents

Acknowledgements

An earlier version of Chapter 5 first appeared as 'Anarchy of the Internet' in *Ends and Means* 1 (1996) and a small part of Chapter 6 first appeared in 'Sex and Violence in Fact and Fiction' in Matthew Kieran (ed.) *Media Ethics* (Routledge, 1998).

Introduction

The scale and speed at which the interconnected forms of electronic communication known variously as the Net, the Internet, the World Wide Web or cyberspace have entered ordinary life in almost all its aspects is very striking. But, despite its popularity and the rate at which its use has spread, it is still very new, too new in fact to allow much in the way of retrospective reflection on its nature and impact. Even so, its importance can hardly be denied and consequently the impulse to try to think about what it is and what it may mean for culture, law and politics is very great. Anyone who undertakes to write about it in a reflective vein, however, must accept that both the technology and its use are sure to alter considerably even while such reflection is taking place. The result is that writing about the Internet (the term I shall generally use), even if it is neither merely descriptive nor technical, faces the risk of being out of date even before it reaches the bookshops. A book such as this, then, is a chancy undertaking.

The prospect of its relevance is further threatened by its being an essay in philosophy. In the world of information technology the Internet is the newest of the new; amongst forms of reflection philosophy is the oldest of the old. Is it likely that familiarity with the age-old questions of philosophy will throw much light on the latest technological innovation? The answer to this question is one for the reader to judge, but arriving at a judgement on it may be assisted by a few introductory remarks designed to make clear the nature of the exercise in hand.

This short book is a philosophical exploration. It is not an account of the history of the Internet and its development. Nor does it aim to get people 'on' to it. Although what it has to say will inevitably be of greatest interest to those who regularly use the Internet, it *assumes* no special interest in using the Internet, still less any expertise on its use. Where it seems necessary for the benefit of the general reader, I shall provide some basic information about what it is and how it works (all of it very familiar to most readers no doubt). But the point of view the book adopts is not that of the user of the Internet, whether enthusiastic or reluctant; rather, it is the point of view of those who live in the social and cultural world into which the Internet has sprung. And of course this means nearly all of us. The central questions are: what should we think about this new phenomenon? Is it really a truly novel development? Should we fear it, or welcome it with open arms?

To almost anyone, I imagine, these will seem natural questions to raise. But why deploy philosophy in attempting to answer them? The answer is that the book aims to identify some of the issues which the advent of the Internet, albeit at an early stage of its development, throws upon our attention. These are the issues which concern us as communicators, learners, parents, teachers, lawmakers and citizens, both national and global, and these very general categories are those in which philosophy is perennially interested and to which its two millennia of thought are relevant. In fact, as I hope to show, making a provisional assessment of the nature and implications of the Internet cannot but involve us rapidly in some of the questions with which social philosophy, ethics, moral psychology and the philosophy of education are traditionally concerned.

There is a further point to be made in favour of such a study. New as the Internet is, it has already prompted a number of books which aim to move beyond explaining and exploring its uses to reflect on its nature and impact. Many of these are expressions of fearfulness, even those written by experts in its technology. But relatively few, if any, have called upon the resources of a long-standing, not to say ancient, discipline of inquiry, and as a result they have tended to be personal and impressionistic rather than systematic. Philosophy has this to offer: it does not content itself with the merely impressionistic or opinionated. What it aims to supply is a critical assessment based upon argument structured in accordance with age-old canons of reasoning. This, in my view, lends it a certain kind of rational authority and allows it to pass beyond the simple expression or exchange of beliefs and opinions, however heartfelt and well informed.

Still, the necessarily provisional nature of any such assessment at the present time is undoubtedly a limitation. But something significant will have been achieved if we can determine with reasonable clarity just what the issues are and what moral and conceptual ramifications they may have. To achieve this it is necessary to set the examination of issues specific to the Internet in the wider context of the philosophy of technology, which is to say, within an understanding of the place of technology within human culture as a whole, its relation to knowledge, political decision-making and the achievement of human goals. It is with the philosophy of technology in general that the first three chapters are principally concerned, and this is why they contain relatively little direct discussion of the Internet. But by embedding questions about the Internet in the broader framework of the philosophy of technology, we can go some considerable way towards identifying the main issues relevant to its advent. Subsequent chapters deal directly with the Internet itself, but even here, bearing in mind the speed and unpredictability of its development, the main aim is to identify in advance those places in which to keep looking as the changing nature of the Internet unfolds. There is no attempt in these later chapters to make speculative guesses about the future, always an intellectually fruitless endeavour in my view, but rather to establish a framework of understanding with which to think about whatever hitherto unimagined novelties the Internet throws up next.

The stimulus to undertake such a task, and the ability to make some headway with it, derives from my taking responsibility for the Centre for Philosophy, Technology and Society at the University of Aberdeen in 1996. The CPTS, as it is known locally, was established in 1990 through the initiative and foresight of some of my colleagues, especially Dr Nigel Dower, its first Director. The interests of the Centre range over the full spread of modern technological innovation, medical and environmental as well as electronic, but we were able to take a special interest in information technology thanks to a generous grant from the Scots Philosophical Club. This allowed us to establish an interdisciplinary inter-university research group on 'The Moral Implications of Information Technology'. The group, which has met regularly since then, focused fairly speedily on the Internet, and the implications equally speedily proved to be wider than 'the moral' might imply, at least if this is narrowly conceived. The group included specialists in public policy, sociology, theology and film studies as well as philosophers, and I must record here the great benefit I have derived from its discussions and deliberations. Indeed, without it I should have nothing to say on these matters.

Another such debt lies in an invitation by BBC Radio Scotland to write and present a series of four programmes under the title 'The Silicon Society'. These were broadcast in May 1997, and I am most grateful to their producer Declan Lynch both for the requirement to put my thoughts in a more concise and accessible form and for the interesting material he assembled in his interviews with a large number of people across the country. The series, I should add, followed on from the prize-winning 'Kane Over America', produced by Ian Docherty, another BBC Radio Scotland programme which provided me with material to think about.

That earlier programme included an interview with Neil Postman, Professor of Communications at New York University and author of *Technopoly*. Interviewed by Pat Kane, Postman offers us a test by which we might assess the usefulness of technological innovation. He invites us to ask of any piece of new technology – what is the problem to which this is a solution?

> I recently went to buy a car, a Honda Accord, I don't know if you know this, it's a very good Japanese car, and the salesman told me that it had cruise control and I asked the salesman this question, which took him by surprise. I said: 'What is the problem to which cruise control is the solution?' Well, apparently no one had ever asked him this question before, so he pondered it for a bit, and then he said, as his face brightened, 'Well, it's the problem of keeping your foot on the gas'. And I said, 'Well, I've been driving for 35 years, and I've never really

found that a problem'. So then he said, 'Well, you know, this car also has electric windows'. So, you know what I asked him – 'What is the problem to which electric windows are the solution?' and he was ready for me this time. He said, 'Well, it's the problem of having to wind the windows up and down with your arm', so I said 'Well, I never really found that a problem. As a matter of fact, as an academic, I live a rather sedate life and I like the exercise of moving my arms occasionally'. Well, the point is I bought the Honda, and with cruise control and with electric windows, because you cannot buy a Honda Accord without cruise control and electric windows, whether you wish to or not. Now that first raises an interesting question, which is that technology, while it obviously increases options in many instances, also frequently limits options. People who are very enthusiastic about technology are always telling us what it will do for us. They almost never address the question of what it will undo.

Postman's question is one which there is reason to examine more closely, and we will return to it and to his more subtle analysis in *Technopoly*. But behind the question as it stands is this thought: are we really better off for having the latest gadgets? 'The latest gadgets', of course, is a pejorative way of describing them, and to some people it bespeaks a cast of mind that is aggressively anti-technological and anti-progressive. Indeed, Postman's strictures on technological innovation have been described, and dismissed, in just these terms. What we encounter here, I think, is a disagreement between different ways of thinking about technology. This disagreement is now quite widely described as that between Neo-Luddites and Technophiles. It is this terminology I shall employ and with this disagreement that I shall begin.

1 Neo-Luddites versus Technophiles

The origins of Luddism

In the early nineteenth century the followers of Ned Ludd (according to some his name was actually Ludlum) smashed machinery in factories across Yorkshire and Nottinghamshire, fearing that these new devices would destroy their jobs and livelihood. Whatever the justice of their cause and the truth of their contentions, they paid very dearly for their actions, being subsequently tried and hanged. However, in hindsight what is more striking than the savage way they were treated, common enough at the time unfortunately, is the marked futility of their attempt to stop the new technology of textile manufacture from radically altering the world, not only of textiles, but of industrial production at large. Ludd and his companions, we might say, were engaged in fighting the future, and so described this was a battle that was bound to end in defeat, as now seems obvious. Their major contribution to history, in fact, was to provide a name – Luddites – for all those who hopelessly and fruitlessly resist and oppose technological innovation.

The Luddites were neither the first nor the last such protesters. Tailors who had welcomed the advent of machine-produced cloth, only a few years later smashed the still more innovative technology of Barthelemey Thimonnier, an early French inventor of the sewing machine. Likewise, the growth and development of information technology, at a prodigious rate in recent years, has produced a Neo-Luddite reaction – the term Luddite being deployed in this context with a small measure of pride by Ian Boal in a book (partly) entitled *Resisting the Virtual Life*. Another self-confessed Neo-Luddite is the essayist and conservationist Wendell Berry, author of 'Why I Am Not Going to Buy a Computer' in which (as the title suggests) he defends the retention of old methods and decries the deleterious effects of the new. Like the original Luddites, opponents of computers and the Internet often make predictions about the dire effects of these new ways of doing things – for instance that book-reading will become a thing of the past, that personal communication will cease to be face to face, that future generations will be computer junkies, 'amusing themselves to death' (the title of another book by Postman), or that a new and anarchical form of radical social isolation has come into view as individuals live more and more in their own self-chosen (and fantastical) worlds of virtual reality.

Undoubtedly the most dramatic (and unpleasant) recent expression of Neo-Luddism is that of the Unabomber, so-called because his campaign against modern technology took the form of posting bombs to universities and airlines. The Unabomber preserved his anonymity for several years, but was eventually identified as Dr Theodore Kaczynski, a brilliant mathematician who, after a brief academic career, retired to a cabin in Montana from which he pursued his campaign against modern technology. In 1995, under pressure from the US Attorney General, the *Washington Post* and the *New York Times* published his manifesto: 'Industrial Society and the Future'. This triumph led, ironically, to his detection, arrest and conviction, but as Kujundzic and Mann have pointed out, it is easy to dismiss the document as the ravings of a madman because of the violence and destructiveness of his campaign. In fact he gives cogent expression to a Neo-Luddism which is more widely held and deserves serious attention. According to Kaczynski:

> The industrial revolution and its consequences have been a disaster for the human race. They have greatly increased the life-expectancy of those of us who live in 'advanced' countries, but they have destabilized society, have made life unfulfilling, have subjected human beings to indignities, have led to psychological suffering in the Third World (to physical

suffering as well) and have inflicted severe damage on the natural world.

(Kujundzic and Mann, p. 12)

These are serious charges, and Kaczynki's manifesto (regardless of his methods) makes a not inconsiderable defence of them. But even if in the end we dismiss it, there are more modest voices to be contended with. In a much less general and much less apocalyptic form, Neo-Luddism often contents itself with doubting whether the new technology of the computer and the Internet really does bring greater benefits, whether, that is to say, we are in fact better off than we were before its advent. This is the general direction of Berry's objections, in fact.

Is there any truth or substance in either version of the Neo-Luddites' view? It is notable that even plausible predictions about the effects of new inventions can turn out, in retrospect, to be ludicrous. John Phillip Souza – the composer who was to the march what Strauss was to the waltz – regarded the introduction of the phonograph with great foreboding: 'I foresee a marked deterioration in American music and musical taste, an interruption in the musical development of the country, and a host of other injuries to music in its artistic manifestations, by virtue – or rather by vice – of the multiplication of the various music-producing machines' (quoted in Boorstin, *The Americans: The Democratic Experience*, p. 657). Ninety years later, the survival of traditional instruments and the vigorous state of music-making makes such a remark appear ridiculously wide of the mark. Still, one point worth making is that the predictions Luddites make may sometimes come true – what the future holds is always hard, perhaps impossible, to say. Moreover it is plausible to think that in several cases their estimates of cost over benefit are correct. This second possibility, that new technology does not in fact bring a net benefit, is a claim to which we will return, but what is more interesting for present purposes is that even the accuracy of their predictions, which only the actual course of the future can confirm or refute of course, does little to alter the futility of Luddism. Whatever the elegance and attractiveness of the fountain pen or the typewriter, it seems

certain that, *pace* Berry, widespread use of the information technology of the computer is here to stay (and set to expand) in as yet
unforeseeable directions. As has often been said in other connections – nuclear power or genetic manipulation, for instance – what
has been invented cannot be uninvented, and once invented someone somewhere will want to use it and succeed in doing so. In the
case of the Internet, there is no need to speculate on 'someone,
somewhere'. Such large numbers of people, everywhere as it seems,
have taken it up that we can be sure it will not go away. At the
same time, to declare all doubts and questions about the Internet
to be Luddite, is to run the danger of falling victim to the other
extreme, an extreme we might call 'the ideology of technology'.

Technophilia

The 'ideology of technology' is most evident in Technophiles:
those who believe that technological innovation is a cornucopia
which will remedy all ills. 'Technophiles' is a term coined by Neil
Postman and he defines such people as those who 'gaze on technology as a lover does on his beloved, seeing it without blemish
and entertaining no apprehension for the future' (Postman,
Technopoly, p. 5). Along with Postman, I shall have more that is
critical to say about this sort of technophilia, but to anyone who
observes the matter with reasonable impartiality it is an important
fact, and one to be accommodated, that computers and comput-
ing generate a striking degree of enthusiasm. When the World
Wide Web was first being developed, for example, a large number
of very talented people became engrossed in the technical problems it gave rise to and devoted a huge amount of time and talent
to producing solutions which they freely released into the world of
cyberspace. They did so, however, not so much (if at all) because
they were enthused by the project of creating a vast international
system of communication and exchange, still less because they had
weighed up the pros and cons, the costs and benefits of such a system. Their motivation lay, rather, in the fact that they were in-
trigued by the technical problems. This is one aspect of the
ideology of technology – technological problem-solving becomes
an end in and of itself, irrespective of larger considerations. Or, to

put the matter more accurately, the question of means is the dominant (even sole) consideration and the question of the value of ends to which they are the means is left to take care of itself.

A second important aspect of the ideology of technology is its assumption that the most technologically advanced is the best. This might be taken as the defining characteristic of technophilia, in fact. It is also the belief that (according to Postman) has ushered in 'Technopoly', a world ruled by technological innovation. He contrasts the modern world, especially in America, with earlier 'tool using' societies. In these, technology was the servant of other independent purposes, and regulated by them. Technopoly, by contrast 'eliminates alternatives to itself' (Postman, *Technopoly*, p. 48). Postman, in my view, generalizes and dramatizes too much, but he does identify an important assumption that accompanies a great deal of modern technology – that all that went before is redundant and to be discarded because inferior. Allied with it is a further, almost equally important, assumption – that countries and individuals who want to increase or preserve their prosperity must invest heavily in hi-tech. This explains both the increasing number of government initiatives which aim to make everyone computer literate and the widespread introduction of in-service IT training courses. The desirability of such initiatives rests upon several unexamined suppositions. Chief among these are two ideas, first, that the source of the ends which technology serves lies elsewhere than in the sort of intellectual inquiry and imagination which technological invention itself requires (in consumer demand, perhaps, which in turn is thought of as simply the reflection of individual desires) and, second, that technology is neutral with respect to those ends – it merely serves them (or fails to do so) and does not influence or determine them.

These assumptions, in my view, make the ideology of technology very powerful and help to explain why opposition to technological innovation is easily dismissed as Luddism. Yet it is not difficult to find evidence that under the influence of an unquestioning ideology of technology, large errors have indeed been made, and made in the recent past. Some of these rest upon false predictions, many have involved considerable, but unnecessary expenditure, and all of them have, in one way or another, been a waste of time. Nor are such objections forthcoming only from those who have failed to master the technology of the new way. On the contrary, some of the gravest doubts come from those who know it from the inside. Clifford Stoll, for instance, one of the pioneers of the Internet, has written a book entitled *Silicon Snake Oil* and significantly subtitled *Second Thoughts on the Information Highway*. In it he records very many ways in which this highly advanced technology is used for the most trivial, and trivializing, of purposes, to the point where the degree of sophistication in the means and the lack of it in the ends takes on the character of a gross absurdity.

Some of the sort of doubts Stoll has we will return to. The point to draw from his making them is that they are not the doubts of a technological ignoramus. But even those much less expert than Stoll can see that IT has not always realized the predictions of its enthusiasts. One very familiar example is the 'paperless office'. In the preface to his acclaimed book *Why Things Bite Back*, Edward Tenner records how when personal computers first appeared

> Futurism was thriving. Its most successful practitioner, Alvin Toffler, had declared in his best-selling *The Third Wave* that 'making paper copies of anything is a primitive use of [electronic word-processing] machines and violates their very spirit'. Yet the paper recycling bins seemed always to be brimming with printouts, and even after the office was networked and electronic mail had replaced hard-copy memos, the paper deluge continued ... Networking had actually multiplied paper use. When branches of Staples and OfficeMax opened near Princeton, the first items in the customers' view (and in the catalogues) were five-thousand-sheet cases of paper for photocopiers, laser printers and fax machines.
>
> (Tenner, p. ix)

A related but in many ways more important example is the home office. Telephone lines and computer terminals make it possible for office workers to be linked just as effectively if they are miles apart as if they are in the same room. So people do not need any longer to go *out* to work and can as a result locate themselves wherever they choose. The time of the home-based worker may yet come, but for over a decade now it has been predicted that, as people acquire more IT skills and equipment becomes more widely and more cheaply available, the days of the traditional workplace are numbered. Yet the proportion of the workforce working from home is small and to date shows relatively little sign of growing. The fact appears to be that most people want to work with other people face to face, they want a workplace to go to, a company of fellow workers to belong to and they are willing to pay the price of commuting back and forth in order to have it. Against these facts about human beings, many training initiatives that increase IT skills are for the most part worthless. They have not, and probably will not, lead to the maximization of hi-tech communication, because their doing so conflicts with the patterns of social life that people are disposed to retain.

This feature of the home office and the 'virtual company' (one in which everyone works from home electronically networked to everyone else) is one of the sources of the 'discontent' described by Ellen Ullman in *Close to the Machine: Technophilia and Its Discontents*. Ullmann describes her experience of her 'virtual' software company worked from home.

> Most of all, I had to accept that I was now on my own. The place I had come to before, and would come to again: alone. After two weeks of intense interaction with the programmers at the net-working software company, the true nature of my new contract became clear. I sat in my loft all day staring into my computer. I designed software. Now and then, I sent the designs to the programmers by e-mail or fax. Once or twice a week, I drove down to their office through traffic made hellish by road construction. My most intense relationship became the one with my car.
>
> (Ullman, p. 125)

There are no doubt compensations to 'home offices' and 'virtual companies' but most people, I imagine, would react as Ullman did, and for this reason there is a check on how far such developments are likely to go. Such, at any rate, is a plausible hypothesis. It does not follow that present patterns of work will always remain. After all, there is an historically recordable shift in the other direction; the original Luddites were in part resisting the move from home-based small-scale production to factory-based mass production, which nevertheless came to be the order of most people's lives. Still, what the example of the home office shows is that the value of technology in some part derives from the ends it serves, and if the advance of technology tends to serve ends that run counter to those that will readily be adopted by people at large, technological innovation can be imaginative and dynamic without being useful or valuable. In which case, it is simply costly.

There is, as I have observed, an assumption on the part of the Technophile that the value of technology is neutral. Technophiles tend to believe that the latest device is more efficient, but in so believing they assume that the value of some piece of technology is wholly derived from the purpose it serves; if new technology serves some such purpose better than that which it threatens to replace, then it is to be welcomed. This truth of this, if true it be, does not imply of course that every and any innovation is valuable. Only if we hold the further supposition that later is inevitably better, and hence that the latest is the best, could we justifiably draw this further inference. But, more fundamentally, the supposed neutrality of technology seems easy to refute. Consider in illustration of this the technology of transport. It is by now a commonplace that the building of better cars and better roads – freeways, *Autobahnen* or motorways – has a decided effect upon the demand for these things. It does so by influencing the ends to which they are put. New roads, which are intended to ease the flow of traffic and reduce journey times, almost always lead to *greater* traffic congestion and *longer* journey times. Why is this? The answer is not far to seek. Journeys which were less readily undertaken with less efficient cars and poorer roads, become (in prospect) less daunting if we have the use of better cars and roads. Accordingly many more people are willing to undertake them. But this fact itself induces a great increase in the number of motorists, which in turn undermines the very advantage which the technological advances promised. It is a salutary statistic that journey times in central

London (and many other places) are now no better than they were one hundred years ago, and this despite the enormous technical advances in transport that have been made within that period.

Critical realism about technology

Doubts about the value of technological innovation are not without substance, therefore, and the examples which support them could be multiplied indefinitely. At the same time, it seems plain that setting one's face against modern technology is, in a deep sense, to be at odds with reality. A devoted attachment to the quill pen and the oil lamp, so to speak, flies in the face of history, whatever the respective merits of these particular devices. If so, how are we to avoid the futility of Luddism and at the same time escape the ideology of technology? In a way this is the central question of this book, though its concerns are focused on information technology and in particular the dramatic innovation of the Internet or World Wide Web. The answer can only emerge from a critical examination of some of the conceptual and evaluative assumptions that underlie this new technology. In short, there is a crucial role here for the philosophy of technology and, as I hope to show, this is not a new discipline but the investigation of age-old philosophical questions in a new context.

Before the philosophy proper begins, however, we need to be reminded of some relatively simple facts. The first of these is that technological advances are, in a sense, self-undermining and this inevitably lends them a measure of transience. That is to say, the technological advances of one era generate the ideas and tendencies which come to replace them in the next. It is an outcome that is repeatedly found even in technological advances which are dramatic and widespread in their effect, a truth illustrated again and again in the history of technology. By and large we remember the successes, the things that made a difference. What all but the historians forget are the blind alleys and the total failures. However, just as easily forgotten is the relative transience of even the most influential technology. The United States (like many other parts of the world) was utterly transformed, economically, socially and politically, by the development of rail transport. The owners of railways became the most powerful people in the country, the great railway hubs grew to be centres of civic and commercial life. At one time the economic health of the country rose and fell in almost perfect line with the state of the railways. Then, in a few short years, the train was superseded by the car and the aeroplane, and (at least in the United States) it remains today in a state of dilapidation from which there is good reason to think it will never recover anything of its former importance and prestige.

The steam train, like every other human invention, brought in its wake the enthusiastic, the cautious, the fanatical and the Luddite – *all* of whom were both vindicated and refuted to some degree. Similarly nuclear technology, one of the greatest innovations of the mid-twentieth century, was hailed by some as a source of energy that would save the world, and by others as an uncontrollable power that would destroy it. For a variety of reasons the contribution of nuclear power stations to the world's energy requirements is limited and declining, and the threat of nuclear war which so dominated human consciousness during the Cold War period has receded with unpredictable, and unpredicted, speed. We know now that both the greatest fears and the greatest hopes did not come to pass, though the technology is still with us and unlikely to disappear.

So too, we may suppose, with information technology. The world is indeed being altered by it and will continue to be. But the scale and depth of the alteration, we have every reason to think, will not be of the sort that either optimists or pessimists predict, and the self-appointed task of this book is to explore the perennial issues which need to be understood if we are to make a reasonable assessment of its value and significance. Steering a reasoned middle course between Luddism and technophilia requires the following: that we are not swayed by technological innovation for no better reason than that it is innovatory, and that at the same time we remain open to its actual character and possible advantages. In short we must be alive both to the possibility that computerized information technology may be a truly new way of doing things with real increases in value for those individuals and societies who adopt it, and to the possibility that its novelty and its advantages have been exaggerated. To steer this middle course successfully involves a critical consideration of some crucial assumptions. The purpose of this first chapter is to identify the issues involved in such a consideration and the purpose of subsequent chapters is to examine them in more detail.

Surveying the issues

Is information technology just another tool – more complex and sophisticated, no doubt, but nevertheless not fundamentally different to the flint arrowheads with which people of the Stone Age were enabled to turn from gathering food to hunting it? There is a danger that this question sounds antediluvian, itself the kind of Luddism expressed in the familiar saying 'there's nothing new under the sun'. In fact it can be taken to point to a matter of the greatest importance if we are to take stock of the Computer Age and what is really means. Just how novel is the Internet? Is it simply another way of doing things that we have always done – only better, quicker and cheaper – or is it a wholly new form of communication and human interaction? To the Technophiles, as it seems to me, the Internet represents the beginning of a brave new world. That it is new can hardly be in doubt, at one level, but is it *radically* new? To answer this question we need to say something about the mark of the radically new. Not all novelties are of equal significance. Nothing much turns on the language we use here, but I shall refer to what I think can be regarded as an important difference by contrasting the 'new' with the merely 'novel'. That there is such a difference seems easy to establish. For instance, at some point 'roast beef and mustard' was an unavailable artificial flavour, but its novelty is to be contrasted with the original introduction of the truly new technology which first made available artificially contrived flavours. Such flavours are new, in my terminology, whereas one more is a mere novelty. This distinction between 'the new' and 'the novel', and its application to the Internet, is the subject of Chapter 2.

A second assumption awaiting further examination is one on which something has already been said – the relation between technology and the ends it seems to serve. Here the doctrine of neutrality is central. This doctrine, as it seems to me, is shared in equal measure by (some) Technophiles and Luddites; dissenters can be found in both camps. The idea is that new technologies enter a world of fixed purposes and values, and the question then is whether they serve these purposes and values better or less well, whether they advance them, make no difference or even retard them. On this view human beings seek and have always sought such things as health, prosperity, entertainment and education. To assess the value of technology, therefore, we need only to ask whether or not it more adequately puts these things within our grasp. What this way of thinking excludes, however, is the possibility that technological innovation might not merely alter but *transform* the world with which we are familiar – which is to say, transform the ends we seek and thus the values we espouse – by altering our conceptions of what health, entertainment and so on, are. The dissenters, by contrast, suppose the contrary: on the Luddite side they think that some technologies can and will bring an end to 'civilization as we know it'; on the Technophile side the claim is that new worlds await us or, more vulgarly, that 'you ain't seen nothing yet'.

That some technologies have transformed the world in this sense is a plausible historical claim, and one which we will explore further. Here it is sufficient to note the possibility and to note further that this considerably enlarges the question of value. If technology on occasions does not merely alter but transforms the world, we need to ask not only whether it enables us to do better the things we have always done, but whether the new things it enables us to do make for a better world. This and the previous question are obviously connected. A mark of the new as opposed to the merely novel might lie in precisely this fact – that the new does not simply alter, but transforms. Consequently, after an initial examination of the question 'Is the Internet truly new?', we will have to ask the question 'Is the transformation it promises an improvement or a deterioration in human life?' This is the subject of Chapter 3.

This question, too, has a wider and a narrower interpretation. There are aspects of life which might be transformed, and not merely altered, that are nonetheless aspects too confined or parochial to allow the transformation to count as major. For instance, it might be claimed that television transformed the world. But if this transformation were restricted to the world of entertainment, say, the transformation would itself be importantly limited. The place of entertainment in human life is not to be underestimated – only a certain sort of Puritanism would be inclined to dismiss it as essentially trivial. Nevertheless, were entertainment to be transformed, and the worlds of politics, religion, science, medicine and the family to remain unchanged, the transformation in modes of entertainment could hardly count as a major event in the history of humankind. This is because entertainment, I shall for the moment assert, is a peripheral aspect of existence. There is more to be said about this but, if it is true, a profound transformation involves, consequently, several and specific aspects of existence. Those who believe that the Internet constitutes a transforming technology generally recognize this. They claim that its power ranges not simply over entertainment but over the future of education and, more strikingly, the fabric of social and political life. Among their suggestions is that the Internet has altered or has the power to alter dramatically the exchange of information for academic and scientific purposes. This introduces a new level of significance. If it is true, as several governments appear to believe, that educational methods can be revolutionized by means of the Internet, we can expect the formative influences on new generations to be quite different to those which formerly prevailed. Once again, this is a topic which will concern us at intervals in subsequent chapters.

But yet more important is the claim that the Internet brings with it the possibility of new political forms, most notably the final realization of democracy proper. Via the Internet, not a few people suppose, the will of the people can be expressed and hence effected more efficiently than ever before without economic distinction or social distortion. A related though somewhat different contention is that with the Internet there has arisen the possibility of self-forming communities, communities constituted by self-selected interests and indifferent to customary and international boundaries. On the other side, some see in the Internet an incipient anarchy which subverts both national boundaries and social control, a contention which the more salacious uses of the

Internet tends to confirm. All these are important contentions of very great interest. Part of this interest is that they claim for the Internet the power to create what it would not be an exaggeration to call new worlds, that is to say, new political, moral and communal worlds.

But if such new worlds are in the making, how are we to relate them to those which some think they will replace? The possibility of anarchy – that is to say, a realm beyond the reach of government – is an alluring prospect for some and a social threat of the greatest magnitude to others. These two conceptions of anarchy, the positive and the negative, will provide us with further subjects for investigation. Both rest equally upon the contention, however, that such a thing is possible – that the world of the Internet could become a world beyond political control. Is this true? It is already apparent to many that the Internet has its downside – that it can be used to assist the terrorist, the fraudster and the pornographer, no less than the teacher and the doctor, and these are activities which several governments have set themselves to detect and legislate against. Can it be done? If it can, then the prospect of a new and anarchic world immune to all such regulation, whether it is regarded with pleasure or fear, must be seen to recede. Indeed, another, different prospect comes into view: the Internet could become an instrument of government more powerful and intrusive than any yet encountered. In this scenario it is not the future of government and politics that is called into question, but the privacy of the individual.

These topics – the relation between the state and the individual – far from being new, are the stock-in-trade of centuries of philosophical analysis and argument. In Chapters 4, 5 and 6 they will occupy us in a new connection, but, as we shall see, the issues the Internet raises are not so far from traditional debates which may thus be made to throw some light in this context also.

Even with the prospect of perfect democracy, anarchic freedom and the formation of new communities, the ambitions of the Technophiles and the fears of the Luddites are not at an end. Most dramatic of all is the suggestion that we are on the verge of a new kind of reality – virtual reality – in which we will become possessed of the power to create for ourselves a world of experience which is free from the limits of ordinary contingency, a world in which (for example) I shall be able to climb the Eiger or travel in space without the risks and costs of doing so which have been attached hitherto. To the Technophiles, this is a world of almost unimaginable riches; to the Luddites, it is the final retreat into delusion. Our task here is to arrive at a reasonable adjudication between the dreams and the fears.

With the concept of virtual reality we arrive at the apotheosis of the Internet, and at the final chapter. My own ambition is partly to set out the issues as clearly as I can and to adduce the most cogent arguments on each of the opposing sides so that readers may arrive at their own conclusion. This could properly be deemed sufficient reason for a book of this sort. Assessing the significance of the Internet is a transparently important task at the present time. But I have a further aim: to show that despite (or perhaps because of) its ancient lineage, philosophical reasoning in the Socratic tradition is the best means of doing so – to show, in short, that philosophy is of contemporary and not merely antiquarian interest. Both aims can best be served by proceeding with this question: just how new is the Internet?

2 The radically new and the merely novel

How transformative is the Internet?

> Here is an enormous incalculable force … let loose suddenly upon mankind; exercising all sorts of influences, social, moral and political; precipitating upon us novel problems which demand immediate solution; banishing the old before the new is half matured to replace it; … Yet, with the curious hardness of a material age, we rarely regard this new power otherwise than as a money-getting and time-saving machine … not many of those … who fondly believe they can control it ever stop to think of it as … the most tremendous and far-reaching engine of social change which has ever blessed or cursed mankind.
>
> (Quoted in Boorstin, *The Americans: The National Experience*, p. 581)

The quotation above could plausibly be applied to the Internet. In fact, these remarks were made in 1868 by Charles Francis Adams, Jr, and they refer to the advent of transcontinental railways. The point of noting this striking parallel is not that people repeatedly have the same anxieties, or that they are forever issuing the same warnings with each new wave of technology, but that in every generation some innovations are and can be expected to be of far greater consequence than others. Adams' remarks would be quite out of place applied to, say, the electric shaver, useful and novel though that device has been.

What is the difference? One answer is that the railways were, and the Internet may be expected to be, *transforming* in their impact on the character of personal and social life across a wide range. This is one way of characterizing the difference and what we need to inquire is whether this idea of 'transforming' technologies is sufficient to establish and explain the sort of distinction I set out in the last chapter – that between the radically new and the merely novel. And if it is, what we want to know further is whether there is reason to class the Internet among those technological innovations, like the railways, which are transforming.

The nature of the Internet

In assessing the newness of the Internet, the first step must be to describe it. This is harder than might be supposed because, so rapidly developing is the technology, new uses and features are emerging almost daily. The Internet began life, curiously, as a US military communications system. Its purpose was to provide a wholly secure means by which secret information could be circulated, a kind of internal electronic postal system. This system was extended into the world of academia, where 'gopher' software was developed to assist students in their search for information. It then received an enormous fillip from scientific researchers at CERN, the nuclear research centre in Switzerland, who developed the technology of the 'hyper-text link'. Hyperlinks allow an indefinite number of computer databases to be interconnected electronically and thus the information collected on each to be exchanged between all. Thanks to the hyperlink, whatever is on your computer network is equally accessible to mine. Strictly, the Internet and the World Wide Web are not the same thing. The former is a system of electronic intercommunication; the latter is a way of processing and presenting digital information. But the distinction is of increasingly little interest, because the Web has come to dominate the Internet. As Neil Barrett observes, 'The Web has been described as the "killer application" for the Internet: the application that took the Internet from a relative handful of enthusiasts, into the domain of serious, commercial and governmental users' (Barrett, p. 26).

The combination of these two inventions established the basic components of what I shall simply refer to as the Internet. Once commercial companies became convinced both of its value and its saleability, a truly worldwide Web sprang up and by means of it millions of people and organizations have been enabled to communicate and share digitally stored information. Ironically, given its beginnings in military security, the extension of this technology to civilian use has introduced the freest, most lightly regulated, most international communications system in the history of mankind, and it was rapidly in the interests of software companies to make widely available programmes which gave the most ordinary of their customers entry to it.

The most immediately useful aspect of the Internet is the electronic mail system known as e-mail, which combines features of post, fax and telephone at relatively little cost. Its ease and immediacy has made it attractive to huge numbers of users very rapidly. The Internet or Web (properly so-called) is much more than this, however. It brings together the features of a vast library, a gigantic picture gallery, a worldwide noticeboard, and it is increasingly the primary vehicle for large numbers of intercommunicating and interactive interest groups. An inestimable amount of information is available on it. Many millions of images can be found there, ranging from Old Masters through full-colour advertisements and moving pictures to personal photographs and amateur sketchings. Daily newspapers, academic journals and book-length typescripts can be accessed by means of it. Every conceivable type of interest and activity can now be found to have an Internet group. These serve anything from the most advanced scientific research to the most trivial of hobbies, from the greatest religions to the least savoury of human perversions. It is possible to operate bank accounts, purchase goods, engage in academic exchanges or make travel plans, including booking tickets and even viewing prospective hotel rooms. Friendships are made on the Internet (hourly I imagine) and there are now many recorded instances of the most deeply personal relationships being formed there, relationships which have led to marriages between people who have never encountered each other physically up to that point. Such, it seems, is the dramatic power of the personal computer which, not so long ago, was little more than an advanced typewriter-cum-calculator.

To get some grasp on what the Internet is, then, we need to imagine a combination of library, gallery, recording studio, cinema, billboard, postal system, shopping arcade, timetable, bank, classroom, newspaper and club bulletin. We should then multiply this by an indefinitely large number and give it unlimited geographical spread. Such a thought experiment may help to induce some sense of the size and scope of the Internet, but what it can fail to emphasize is the all-important feature of interaction. Nearly everyone is familiar by now with the phrase 'surfing the Net'. The image is slightly misleading, however. It suggests a passive skimming of the surface of something. In fact, there is life on the Internet in a fairly strong sense. While it is true that the Internet can be used as a source of information, like a vast encyclopaedia, and that it provides a new and valued vehicle for announcements and advertisements, it is far more than this. In short, it is not merely possible to *observe* the world of the Internet; it is possible to *exist* and to *act* in it. It is this that has brought into currency the term 'cyberspace' – an entirely new 'spatial' dimension created by cybernetics, a dimension in which we can have a life.

If 'being' in cyberspace is a new kind of being, distinct from but nonetheless just as metaphysically substantial as 'being' in the flesh for instance, then there can be little doubt that the Internet is indeed a radically new technology. However, I shall leave the critical examination of this very ambitious claim about the newness of the Internet to the final chapter, because it seems clear that claims about the radical newness of the Internet are made, and could perhaps be better founded, upon a less dramatic basis. Whatever may be true about its status as 'a new realm of being', the Internet naturally offers itself for comparison with other major epoch-making inventions – the automobile or the telephone, for instance – and indeed this is a useful way to begin. Is the world we have inhabited until lately, the world without the Internet, a bit like the long-gone world without the motor car?

The radically new and the merely novel

Every year motor car manufacturers present the world with new models. Often these are new not merely in style, but in engineering. It would be impossible to deny that since the internal combustion engine was first invented, motor vehicles have changed and in many respects improved enormously. They are faster, more comfortable, safer and more efficient than ever before. Nevertheless, there seems to be a clear sense in which every new model is only an extension of the original invention, with which the ground-breaking step was made. In my terminology the difference between the two is to be marked by saying that while the original invention was radically new, every subsequent adaptation and improvement, however much it may be welcomed, has been merely novel. In the hyperbolic language of advertisers the latest model may be described as a 'new concept' in engineering, but in fact it was the combination of the private carriage with the internal combustion engine which ushered in a new conception of personal transport. Subsequent changes and improvements do not represent new 'concepts' at all, but rather extensions and refinements of the original innovative idea.

Someone might raise this question: why should we draw the distinction between transformation and extension, between the radically new and the merely novel, at just this point? After all, motor cars were invented in the course of a longer history which we can describe more broadly, namely the history of transportation. The motor car replaced the horse-drawn carriage and was, in certain ways, an advance on the train. Should we not see it as just one more stage in a seamless web of development which, if we go back far enough, began with the invention of the wheel?

Now whatever we make of this particular case, this way of expressing doubts about the distinction between the new and the novel shows how difficult it is to avoid the idea that the history of technology is to be recounted in terms of more and less radical innovations. No one would deny, I imagine, that the invention of the wheel was one of the most significant steps in technological history, a step with consequences far beyond the telling of those who first found a use for it. The wheel is not merely a feature of cars and carriages. It is essential to pulleys and the basis of the cog, and thereby the working principle of clocks and looms and gears. In short, the wheel is crucially involved in machinery of every sort. Architecture, industry and engineering, no less than transportation, are what they are and have accomplished what they have because the wheel was invented, and it is only with the advent of genetic manipulation and the silicon chip that its centrality has been eclipsed to any serious degree.

Still, if reflection on the significance of the wheel convinces us that there is an important distinction between the radically new and the merely novel, it is no less important to decide at which points in an otherwise continuous processes of development the distinction is to be applied. This point can be made about the Internet, or a large part of it at any rate, no less than about the motor car. It is a form of communication which, like printing, depends crucially upon the written word, and for this reason the Internet can be construed as simply one more innovation in a long development which began, in the mists of time, with the invention of writing. Why should we regard its advent as specially important?

What this question shows, in both cases, is that (for most purposes at least) it is only at the cost of distortion that the history of technology can be cut up into discrete segments with clear and identifiable beginnings marked out by single inventions. It does not follow however that this history is a seamless web within which no specially significant points can be isolated. We can agree that technological innovations are rarely (if ever) *de novo* inventions which spring out of nowhere, and still assert that there are more and less important inventions. After all, something of this sort must be said in other, related connections. Newton and Darwin worked within a continuous tradition of inquiry dating back to the Greeks. Yet their ideas stand out and have regularly been recognized as specially significant moments in the history of science. So too in technology. As to which points the specially significant ones are, we must let intuitions guide us here to some degree. In *Novum Organum* Francis Bacon writes:

It is well to observe the force and effect and consequences of discoveries. These are to be seen nowhere more conspicuously than in those three which were unknown to the ancients, and of which the origin, though recent, is obscure; namely, printing, gunpowder, and the magnet. For these three have changed the whole face and state of things throughout the world; the

first in literature, the second in warfare, the third in naviga-
tion; whence have followed innumerable changes.

(Bacon, sect. 129, p. 118)

How do the inventions Bacon cites compare with the invention
of paper, the clock, the telescope or the radio? It is hard to say,
and Bacon may have overstated the case for all or any of the three.
Nevertheless, those he lists and those with which I have invited
comparison, are all plausible cases of highly significant inventions
and *any* of them can be contrasted in this respect with the
Pullman car, the aerosol can or the electric carving knife. Some inventions just *are* much more important than others. The invention
of the jet engine was useful and is notable, yet it can hardly be
ranked alongside the invention of the aeroplane itself, even though
it greatly enhanced the value of the aeroplane as a mode of transport. The mobile phone is an important development with many
consequences, but it must take second place to the original invention of the telephone on which it is a refinement.

In the light of these and many other examples it seems evident
that not all novel technological devices are of equal significance
and this holds true even if we cannot say just which of two inventions was the more important. It must be conceded that the history of technology cannot be sharply divided into periods marked
by being the 'before' and 'after' of some invention, and further
that inventions cannot be classified under just two headings – the
new and the merely novel. For all that, some such distinction is
unavoidable if the history of technology is to be told at all, just as
the history of science requires a distinction between major and mi-
nor discoveries. The more testing question for present purposes is
how it is best explained. What makes a more significant invention
more significant?

Social transformation: using the Marxist model

The electric can-opener, however useful it is and however
widespread it may have become, is not a very plausible candidate
for a major technological innovation; by contrast, the invention of
the wheel was. What we are looking for is the distinguishing mark

by which, in a handy if somewhat hackneyed expression, the second can be said to have 'changed the course of history' while the first cannot. Especially good examples of radical change are to be found in those technological advances which together added up to what we now refer to as the Agricultural Revolution and the Industrial Revolution in Europe of the eighteenth and nineteenth centuries. What made these *revolutions*? Or better, what was it about these technological advances which seems to warrant such a dramatic description? I shall suggest two. First, the changes that are named in this way provided hitherto unimagined ways of fulfilling recurrent human desires. Second, they brought in their wake large-scale alterations in the structure of social and cultural life. It is instructive to consider each of these in turn.

The effect that the Industrial and Agricultural Revolutions had on the food supply, and the supply of other goods and services, rendered (eventually) the provision of human needs easier, more abundant and more reliable than hitherto could have been imagined. Allied to scientifically based technology and developments in transportation, all of which were importantly interconnected of course, the consequences were still greater. For one thing, dependence on local conditions and contingencies of production such as the weather and the supply of raw materials was massively reduced. These new means of production (which have continued to develop into the present age of the disposable) extended to very large numbers of people the means of satisfying basic (and not so basic) desires with far less effort, risk and expense than hitherto, with the result, for one thing, of altering the balance between work and leisure.

To take just one example. The production of cloth before the spinning-jenny and the weaving machine was necessarily small-scale and relatively highly skilled. This limited the amount that could be supplied and hence held the price relatively high. Accordingly, most people were poorly clothed and, as Marx observed, the growth in population added a downward pressure on limited supply. By altering this limit, which is what the invention of textile machinery did, the pressure was eliminated. At the same time substantial surpluses became available for export, thus creating a huge stimulus to international trade. Indeed, if we were to follow Marx's analysis (and in this instance there is some reason to do so), the productive capacity of the new technology, in combination with capital accumulation, removed all effective limits because there came into existence a system of production whose capacity, though not infinite for obvious reasons (the production of everything is limited at some point), was indefinite. From a severely practical point of view, however, indefinite is as good as infinite. I do not need an *infinite* supply of goods to meet my needs; at the very most I only need a supply with no definite limit. The latter is enough to make it limitless in practice. With the advent of production on this scale, any residual poverty is a problem not of the production of goods, but of their distribution. That is to say, continuing debilitating shortages on the part of particular groups and individuals (the poor, the proletariat), which did indeed persist throughout the nineteenth century, had to do with the distribution of wealth – the power to purchase – rather than material availability. Hence the rise of social movements concerned with 'justice' and not merely poverty.

So at any rate Marx contends. His central claim, simplified, is that capitalistic production has the power to supply human need indefinitely, but private ownership of the means of production skews the distribution of wealth so badly that most people cannot actually obtain the goods it produces. I shall not stop to ask here whether Marx was right about this. It is sufficient for my purposes if he is correct in his earlier contention, that the revolutionary or transforming character of the Industrial and Agricultural Revolutions lay in their ability to satisfy recurrent human needs indefinitely and thus transcend the perceptible limitations of all former systems of production. They thus altered both the parameters of human exchange and the perceptions of individuals.

The second (related) feature of such revolutions, also a feature identified by Marx it seems to me, is the widespread change that they brought about in social and cultural life. Marx thought that even the realm of ideas and concepts was among the detectable changes of this sort. His theory of ideology makes a society's political and moral superstructure a product of its material and economic base. It is easy to find examples of precisely the sort of thing he had in mind, but it is hard to sustain the general theory he builds upon them. Even if we reject his very strong version of historical materialism, however, it seems impossible to deny that at many times and in many places social forms and political orders (including social and political ideas) have been significantly altered by new technologies of production. To enumerate only the (now) most commonplace observations: first, the mechanization of agriculture rendered many in the countryside unemployed. This has been exaggerated, no doubt, and it is true that there has been a greater drop in the number of agricultural workers in Europe in *this* century than in the centuries in which what we call the Agricultural Revolution took place (though the explanation may well lie with increasing mechanization and thus confirm the original contention). Nevertheless, the formation and growth of cities is a marked feature of the earlier period and has to be accommodated in any satisfactory account of the historical development of the modern world.

One plausible explanation of the rise of the urban proletariat is that at the same time as employment in agriculture fell, the growth of the factory required for its efficient organization sizeable numbers of workers within relatively easy reach. It was from this, the argument goes, that the growth of cities received a huge stimulus. Added to these social changes was the expansion in population which came about as infant mortality fell and average life expectancy increased. These three forces (and once more I am following Marx) combined to make the vast majority in the nations where such changes took place town-dwellers. Because of this (it is not fanciful to claim) the nuclear family replaced the extended family and increasing numbers of people became detached from the cultural (notably religious) patterns that had up to this point provided the framework of their existence. As a further consequence the political orders which had served those patterns ceased to have much, or indeed any, relevance. The result was that traditional political and social structures had little effectiveness for the majority of people who now lived in towns and cities; they neither reflected nor offered control over the lives people actually led. If this analysis is correct we should expect, and we do indeed find, widespread movements for social and political reform. Supposing Marx to be right, the principal stimulus for these movements was not the rational appeal and consequent spread of liberal democratic ideas, but the changes wrought by new forms of production. The ideas reflected rather than brought about the change.

There is a good deal in this account of the historical development of Europe that might be queried, and Marx's analysis of history has been subject to serious and effective questioning. It is not difficult to substantiate the charge of over-generalization and hence that of simplification. The feudalism of the pre-industrial world was not one thing and the collapse of the social forms characteristic of the European Middle Ages was not uniform. Religious belief, for example, which Marx's analysis implied would decline, seems to have been stronger in the nineteenth century than in the eighteenth in several industrialized countries; and in most of them the state, far from 'withering away' as he predicted, has gone from strength to strength. In the light of these criticisms it must be agreed that Marx's account of history is painted with a very broad brush. Moreover, in common with the other major thinkers of his time, he construes the whole of the past in terms of European history and largely excludes the experience of the non-European world. Nevertheless, Marx's account of the significance of the Agricultural and Industrial Revolutions seems to me to be true in the most general terms and, if it is, this explains what it means to call them *transforming*. For present purposes, this analysis of transformation allows us to make some headway with the subject which is our present concern.

Television as a test case

In the light of the foregoing characterization of what makes technological changes transforming, consider now the 'revolution' in communications which television is commonly said to have heralded. But does television actually provide us with an example of a technological invention which meets these two criteria of significant innovation – the criteria of radical newness? At minimum, a plausible case can be made for saying 'no'.

Take first the supplying of recurrent needs. Let us agree that there is more to life than food and clothing. What is it that television might be thought to provide more abundantly than before?

Obvious suggestions, to which I have already alluded, are information and entertainment. That television supplies these is not in doubt, and with the enormous multiplication of channels promised by the advent of digital television, the sheer amount of entertainment available certainly exceeds anything previous generations imagined. Nevertheless, that it supplies them to a degree that is *qualitatively* and not merely *quantitatively* different from the forms of supply that preceded them seems much more questionable. Indeed, it can plausibly be argued that television has produced *poorer* forms of entertainment than those that came before it, and forms, moreover, which precisely exploit its ability to confuse informing and entertaining. Those 'studio encounter' programmes which have become such a common and popular feature of American television can be interpreted as providing a respectable gloss for the most prurient forms of entertainment by allowing them to masquerade as 'exploratory' and 'investigative' treatments of human emotion and human relationships, when in fact they are arguably the hi-tech equivalent of freak shows. If this is so, a low form of entertainment is being falsely presented as a form of information (and thus education) for no better reason than that it is technically more sophisticated.

A different but related question can also be raised about the relation of even 'straight' news reporting on television to the spread of knowledge and, more importantly, to its social significance. It is certainly true that information about (including pictures of) world events is distributed by TV far more widely and much faster than hitherto. But is this a real improvement in the way that the widespread availability of better and cheaper clothing has been? Whereas better and cheaper clothing transformed the ability of ordinary people to protect themselves and their children against the elements, the fact is that, though far more people are better informed than before, there is relatively little more that they can do with this information. There is every reason to believe that the influence ordinary individuals living in the nineteenth century had over political events, national as well as international, was slight. Arguably, however, this was not a result of their knowing little about them. Had they *known* more, would they have been able to *do* more? If we answer this question in the negative, as there is good reason to do, by parity of reasoning there is no substantial ground to believe that knowing more about events *now* has increased the influence of ordinary citizens on the course of contemporary affairs. 'Knowledge is power' is a familiar slogan (to which we will be returning), but I doubt if there is much truth in it as a generalization. In reality, our greater knowledge of events is as likely to increase our frustration as to increase our power.

The defence of this claim is closely connected with the nature of democracy, a subject which Chapter 4 will examine in more detail, but even in advance of this there would appear to be some ground for the thought that merely knowing more about events is of limited value in terms of personal influence and control. The world is not any more of our making just because we know more about it. Indeed, the very fact that we know more may bring us to a greater realization of how little control we have, which is why I say that 'knowledge is frustration' is an equal contender with the more familiar claim that 'knowledge is power'.

It is important not to be overly cynical about the impact of mass media. Nevertheless, the undoubted ability of television to increase our knowledge is not in itself an unqualified enrichment. A lot of the information conveyed is essentially trivial and trivializing. A slightly different point, but with similar implications, might be made about entertainment proper. Any genuine enrichment in entertainment, widely construed, must show itself, I am inclined to think, in an increase in imaginative power and not merely in wider distribution. The point here is that television may allow us to fill many more hours of leisure time than before, while not enabling us to fill them in noticeably better ways than older forms of entertainment did – folk art and conversation, for instance. We have a greater choice, certainly, if we think of choice on a purely numerical level. But do we have enhanced criteria by which to choose? People whose interests are restricted to what they eat have greater choice if the number of fancy cakes is increased. There is still an important difference to be drawn between them and others who, though they have no more cakes from which to choose, have had their interests extended into local history or music, say. Such people are better off in a way that the former are not.

These remarks are not primarily worth making as substantial contentions about television which it is important to defend, though I believe them to be true by and large. Their role in the present argument is as indicators of a genuine doubt that can be raised about the innovative character of technological advances which have indeed had widespread impact and appeal. Television has had almost unprecedented impact and brought about a degree of international communication in which it is not idle to speak of 'the global village'. But is it truly innovative? Is it a *radically* new form of communication? It could be the case, and indeed may be, that the satisfaction of mass entertainment which television supplies (and it is notable that millions of people can be tuned into the same programme at the same time), makes us no better off (and possibly worse off) than a generation in which equally many millions entertained themselves in a variety of different ways.

Something of the same sort can be said about television with respect to the second criterion of novelty outlined above – impact on social and political forms of life. There is, as it seems to me, no consequence of television that is a clear counterpart to the social and political significance of urbanization. Family life is greatly altered in comparison with times past; this is true. But it is far from obvious that it is television (as opposed to methods of birth control or rising levels of income, say) that has done this. Arguably, television follows social trends; it does not set them. In this respect there is reason to contrast television with the slightly earlier form of mass communication which preceded it, namely radio. A case can be made for saying that radio, which was initially regarded as a medium of entertainment, in fact altered the character of political life, especially in the United States. In particular it ended the role of the public meeting and the place and importance of political oratory within it. One of the great early masters of radio for political purposes was Franklin D. Roosevelt. His Secretary of Labour, Francis Perkins, recalls how the relationship with voters was subtly altered by this medium:

> When he talked on the radio, he saw them gathered in the little parlour, listening with their neighbours … I have sat in those little parlours and on those porches myself during some

of the speeches and I have seen those men and women gathered around the radio, even those who didn't like him or were
opposed to him politically, listening with a pleasant happy
feeling of association and friendship.

(Quoted in Boorstin, *The Americans: The Democratic Experience*,
p. 475)

Radio, in Daniel Boorstin's phrase, 'created the friendly national
politician' in place of the oratorical leader of regional or sectional
interests, and this led to still deeper consequences for the shape
and nature of political life.

> In the totalitarian countries the individual citizen's radio re-
> ceiver, because it was so private a medium, was regarded with
> suspicion as a potential vehicle of treason ... In the United
> States on the other hand, the privacy of radio reception was
> an aid to petty would-be dictators, merchants of hate, and
> demagogues who secured living-room audiences of Americans
> who might have hesitated to attend one of their public rallies.
>
> (Ibid., p. 476)

In short, or so at least there is reason to believe, the invention
of radio changed the workings of politics; F.D.R.'s first inaugural
brought to the White House half-a-million letters, a degree of
popular response and involvement quite unimaginable in Lincoln's
day, one which ended forever the nature of the political order
which extended from Jefferson to Calvin Coolidge (the first broadcasting President), and all thanks to radio. Against this background, there is equal reason to think, television made relatively
little further difference, partly because television much more than
radio is 'a one-way window'; the viewer gets to see what the pro-
gramme-maker chooses to show.

It might be suggested, to the contrary, that this one-way traffic
gave television different, but no less important, political impact.
Even if it has not significantly empowered the populace at large or
substantially enriched their information and entertainment, it has
seriously increased the power of those who rule over them.
Television enables today's rulers to determine political events in a

way that hitherto could be neither contemplated nor attempted. Thanks to the power of the visual it is possible for contemporary governments to manipulate popular opinion in a way that was formerly impossible and in a democracy to command popular opinion is to command political power. Public prominence on this scale, we might say, is political power of a new order.

This is a familiar line of thought, but with respect to it I shall simply record a mild scepticism. It is astonishing (to me) how effectively political control was exercised in the past when distances were, relatively, far greater and systems of communication, by modern standards, unbearably slow. Ancient Rome, after all, successfully ran a very large empire and for over 150 years Britain controlled the subcontinent of India and large parts of Africa to great, if not entirely beneficial, effect. The most geographically widespread empire the world has ever known (the British Empire) knew nothing of television (or radio and telephone, for that matter). On the other side of the comparison it is worth remarking that no convincing evidence has been forthcoming that political campaigns on television are especially effective, partly because it has proved impossible to tell how much televisions, even when they are on, are actually watched. On the contrary, political apathy seems to have grown in the Telecommunications Age. Following the 1997 British General Election, a poll purported to reveal that a staggering 57 per cent of those who had voted claimed to have turned off or changed channels whenever television coverage of the election came on. In the Congressional elections on which President Clinton's impeachment was widely held to turn, only 35 per cent of registered voters bothered to vote. Is it obvious, for all the speed and reach of modern forms of telecommunication, that the power of the modern state is substantially greater than that of the empires of old? Indeed, modern technology may have diminished it, for in a reasonably free society the effect of mass communications is as likely to be the dispersal of power as its concentration, a possibility which Boorstin's observation about radio's assistance to the 'closet' extremist underlines.

This is a point to be dealt with more fully when we address the nature of democracy directly and the potentiality of the Internet with respect to it. For the moment we can rest content with a general scepticism about the social and political significance of television. The upshot of this scepticism is to point to serious doubts about whether the impact of this invention, which has undoubtedly been enormously widespread, amounts to the radically new as opposed to the merely novel. It was radio, not television, which produced a measure of political transformation, or so I have been suggesting, and if this is indeed the case, it illustrates the possibility that technological innovations which attract the most attention are not necessarily those which are the most significant.

Will the Internet transform?

What then of the Internet? The foregoing observations provide a context in which to examine two contentions about it that have been made with sufficient frequency to warrant closer attention, and which relate directly, as it seems to me, to the question of its newness.

Recall the marks of the radically new. We should not allow ourselves to be over-impressed by the popularity and rapid spread of Internet technology, because the same features attended the invention of television about whose significance plausible doubts have been raised. Rather, the marks of a truly transforming technology lie elsewhere and are, I have argued, twofold: the ability to serve recurrent needs better (qualitatively as well as quantitatively) and having a major impact upon the form of social and political life. The first of these – greater ability to serve needs – is in effect an increase in power. With a transforming technology we can do more than previously, and with this increase in power comes an increase in choice. Thus analysed, however, there is a case to be made for the claim that the Internet is a transforming technology, because there is a relation between recurrent needs and the power of choice which can be connected to a notable feature of it. The World Wide Web is power to the people with a vengeance, we might say, since – unlike the rather passive medium of television – its interactive character presents ordinary citizens with the possibility of exercising an unprecedented influence on the social and political events that determine their circumstances and prospects. By dramatically extending their control over these public or communal aspects of their lives it gives them a greater degree of personal autonomy than ever before. Or so it can be and has been claimed. *If* this is true, the Internet thus hugely enhances a value that is fundamental to human life, and thus satisfies a need no less basic than material prosperity.

According to a further line of thought the Internet also satisfies the second criterion of radical newness by presaging a major change in social and cultural forms. It does so by subverting national boundaries. The *worldwide* Web is properly so-called. It has brought into existence a degree of internationalism which is without precedent. By subverting national boundaries it calls into question the power of the state as the dominant force in social life and thus permits the reconfiguration of human communities in line with individually chosen grounds. Such a reconfiguration, should it really come to pass, would be truly transforming because it would make the activities of individuals and groups both indifferent to and subversive of the nation state, an institution around which human life has largely been structured for centuries.

These two purported features of the Internet, its democracy and its internationalism, are characteristics which Chapter 4 will examine more closely. In my view such an examination is central to determining the implications of the Internet, because both are key to the claim that with its creation human beings, thanks to this technological innovation, have entered the realms of the radically new. First, though, more needs to be said about assessing the value of such transformations.

3   The Faustian bargain

Assessing the value of technology

Faust

The story of Dr Faustus has captured many imaginations, most notably of course those of Goethe and Marlowe. A mediaeval legend seems to have got caught up with the real story of a sixteenth-century German necromancer and together they have fashioned the now familiar tale of the man who sold his soul to the Devil in return for unlimited powers, but for a limited time. In Marlowe's version there is considerable pathos in the portrayal of Faustus approaching the end of his twenty-four years as master of all and realizing just what the bargain he had entered into really meant.

It is an image that is easy to apply to technological ambitions. The truly innovative technologist throws himself into a wholly new source of power – electronics, nuclear energy or genetic engineering, say – believing it to contain within it undreamt of sources of power, only to find as the future unfolds that the new technology has its down side, chiefly in the form of consequences which formed no part of the original (invariably over-optimistic) picture. Part of the problem about these Faustian bargains arises from the unpredictability of the future. How can we tell where our inventions will lead? And if we cannot tell this, how can we tell if the benefits will outweigh the costs? In *The Greatest Benefit to Mankind*, his monumental history of medicine, Roy Porter records, again and again, a pattern in which social and commercial advances brought in their wake diseases and epidemics which cut huge swathes through the populations which these advances could have been, and were, expected to benefit. The advent of animal husbandry, for instance, though it secured more reliable sources of food, put people in close proximity to sources of sickness against which they had little natural resistance. Likewise, improved industrial production required a concentration of population which created conditions in which bubonic plague bearing rats could thrive. In fact Porter vividly describes the very development of medicine itself as an unceasing dialectic between the amelioration of known maladies and the consequential rise of new enemies to health.

Every major technological and social innovation, it seems, is attended by unforeseen risks and disadvantages. This is the theme of Edward Tenner's much more wide-ranging study referred to earlier, *Why Things Bite Back*, subtitled *Technology and the Revenge Effect*. Tenner examines four major areas in which technological innovation has been heralded as hugely advantageous and applied with vigour – medicine, agriculture, information processing and sport. In every case he records major deleterious consequences that were wholly unforeseen by the innovators. Some of these outcomes can properly be described as disastrous, yet the unpredictability of the future cannot be allowed to lead us into paralysed inactivity, and rarely has. Life, as we say, tritely but truly, must go on; for both good *and* ill, technology develops and, as Tenner remarks, the slightly boring truth is that 'contemporary technology ... is neither a miracle weapon nor a dud' (Tenner, p. 199).

Still, is there *any* way in which we can adjudicate on such developments before plunging headlong into the latest technological abyss? In the introduction to this book I quoted a radio interview with Neil Postman. Postman offers us a test by which we should always assess the usefulness of technological innovation. Ask of any piece of new technology, he says, what is the problem to which this is a solution? In his book *Technopoly* Postman alerts us to deeper questions of a sort to which we will turn in due course, but in the interview he seems mainly concerned to expose the fact that people can fall in love with the technologically ingenious, or even the merely novel, and under the influence of this technophilia they overlook the all-important business of rationally assessing the value and merits of the technological devices in question. Their love of technology, we might say, is blind. Clearly, since there are such people, his point has rhetorical force. Even so, if we are really interested in such rational assessment, we need to ask: is the question Postman poses a good one?

To arrive at an answer it is necessary to begin by looking at some of its presuppositions. The first is this. As Postman here frames it, the question presupposes that the desire which any technological device aims to serve is prior to and independent of that device. This is even clearer in one of the nine tests for new technology which Wendell Berry offers us in *What Are People For?*: '[any new device] should do work that is clearly and demonstrably better than the one it replaces' (Berry, p. 172). The thought behind both of these tests can be expressed as a variation on David Hume's famous dictum: 'Reason is and only ought to be the slave of the passions' (a dictum that we will have reason to examine directly); technological innovations are and only ever ought to be the slave of independent problems.

Second, Postman's question implies that the problematic character of any task that new technology might enable us to tackle is, so to speak, constituted subjectively. That is to say, a problem is defined as such by whatever we find problematic.

Third, it assumes that technological thinking is purposive through and through, that is, technology can be wholly characterized as means to ends – improved means to an unimproved end, as Thoreau once put it. This third assumption is one so many people share that it might almost be regarded as self-evident. Yet, as I think we shall see, it is an assumption that there is considerable point in questioning. The plan of this chapter, in fact, is to examine each of these assumptions in turn, and then apply some of the conclusions arrived at to thinking about the Internet.

Technology as the servant of desire

Is it true that the need which any technological device is intended to serve exists prior to and independent of that device? There is reason to think not. Postman's question is a natural one, but we might as readily ask of any new piece of technology: what does this make *possible* that was not possible before? This is just as plausible a test for any innovative device, but it is a much less static one; it does not assume a fixed set of desires and purposes. The question about new possibilities is also more in keeping with common experience, since it seems evident that we can and do form new desires and find new interests. In other words, we can *come* to desire things which formerly we did not desire, or even had no idea of desiring. From this fact, a fact which everyday experience appears to confirm, it follows that we can also come to *need* things that formerly we did not need, because, given our newly found desires, we have a use for the means of satisfying them, a use we did not have hitherto, and thus a need for things that we had no need of before.

From what do new desires (and hence new needs) arise? More information is one obvious source. I come to want things that I come to know about. I knew nothing of Chinese food until yesterday, say, but having discovered it, eating Chinese is added to the list of my desires. Now it is important to note that the value of new technology does not depend on the fortuitous advent of new desires. It is not as though desires conveniently spring into existence at the same time as new inventions. The availability of technology has the effect of *stimulating* new desires. I can come to want things not, as it were, directly but because I discover that there are means of accomplishing them. I never thought of holidaying in the Caribbean, let us say, until I discovered the availability of relatively inexpensive flights. Now that it is possible to travel long distances easily and cheaply, I come to want to do it. New technology presents new possibilities, and these new possibilities awaken new desires.

It might seem nonetheless, on further reflection, that the obvious truth of this claim about new desires and the role of technology in helping to form them does not actually contradict the assumption behind Postman's question. So long as wants and desires can be subsumed under general headings – the desire for nourishment, stimulation, entertainment, information, recreation and so on – then technological innovations do not create new desires in any deep or interesting sense. They only open up new ways of satisfying old ones, albeit old ones that admit of greater and more refined specification – holidays abroad and not just holidays, news pictures and not just news, and so on. The point, *contra* my criticism of Postman, is that in as far as these more specific desires can be subsumed under the same general heading, they are not really new. So, for instance, though an open fire and a microwave oven are technologically very different and generate notably different patterns of cooking and entertaining, their value derives from exactly the same underlying source – the desire to cook. Likewise, the appeal of computer games, despite the complex technology which they employ, is not fundamentally different to the appeal of simple board-games like Ludo.

So at any rate it might be claimed, and it is a rejoinder that needs to be examined with care. One thing we can say, however, is that its argumentative strategy – the strategy of subsuming specific needs under general headings – runs the risk of disguising those very differences that there is reason to think present us with genuinely new possibilities. Consider this example. It is plausible to attribute to human beings a general desire to engage in picture-making. In virtually every culture past and present the practice of visual representation can be found, and the cave paintings which archaeologists have uncovered suggest that this is a deep-seated feature of human behaviour which goes back a very long time. Nevertheless, to classify every form of visual art as simply another means of fulfilling this basic inclination involves us in ignoring significant differences between different forms – painting and photography, for instance. Because painting does not have the speed, or cheapness, or power that photography does, it does not allow the ordinary, not specially wealthy, person to make pictures of family outings or a record of their schooldays. These are applications of picture-making which the technology of photography has made possible. We can look back on our past visually, as previous ages did. Nowadays, however, we can relive it in a way that was denied to almost all members of earlier generations, since in the past portrait-painting was largely the preserve of the well-to-do. Furthermore, with the advent of the video camcorder, photography extends to the wealthy and not so wealthy alike a new possibility: re-experiencing the past through moving pictures. Now we can want to do, because we can do, something which previously we could not have wanted, except in the imagination.

The point to be emphasized is that, though the desire to make pictures may indeed be a basic feature of human motivation, the possibility of satisfying it in new and easier ways alters the role of pictures and picture-making in our lives as a whole. Popular photography, indeed, may be said to have *reversed* the relationship between memories and picturing. 'Now, instead of merely photographing persons or scenes that were especially memorable or historic, [people can] photograph at random and then remember scenes *because* they had been photographed. Photography [has become] a device for making experience worth remembering' (Boorstin, *The Americans: The Democratic Experience*, p. 376).

What the example of photography shows is that technological innovation does not always leave the stock of desires as it was. Perhaps it hardly ever does, but almost always alters it by expansion. The invention of electric light was significant at first chiefly as a replacement for the candle and the gas mantle. But it also allowed the development of the spotlight and by extension the projector. In short, the new form of lighting did not merely perform the tasks of the old with greater efficiency and at lower cost: it introduced further possibilities. New technologies can alter the stock of desires at a deeper level also. An implication of the first assumption behind Postman's 'test' question is that the value of technology lies ultimately in its serving certain needs and that these needs can be characterized in an enduring and recurrent way. But in fact there is this further possibility: new technologies can alter our desires by altering our conceptions of those needs. Indeed, elsewhere Postman himself emphasizes precisely this point: 'What we need to consider about the computer has nothing to do with its efficiency as a teaching tool. We need to know in what ways it is altering our conception of learning ... ' (Postman, *Technopoly*, p. 19).

Consider by way of illustration of this the example of health. Eric Matthews has drawn a useful distinction between 'wide' and 'narrow' medical technology, the former referring to practical techniques in general and the latter to techniques devised and constructed from what he calls 'fully scientific' knowledge. Matthews argues that in the case of medical technology, whereas wide technology appeals to an independent general desire for health, the distinguishing mark of the narrow technology of the modern period is the impact it has had on our concept of health. The result is that what human beings conceive of themselves as desiring when they desire a healthy life is different now from what it was in previous periods. It is not merely the means of securing it that have changed, but the thing secured.

> Health comes more and more to mean, not just the normal, species-specific functioning of the human organism (within the constraints of the 'natural order') but the state which medical care ought to achieve for us (which breaks those constraints) ... health becomes, not the best one expects given the limitations of human life, but freedom from those limitations themselves.
>
> (Matthews, in *Ends and Means*, Vol. I, No. 1, p. 20)

I am not here concerned with the cogency of the argument in this particular case, only with its being a plausible exemplar of the idea that the relation between technology and the ends it serves is not as we might naturally assume it to be. The ends we seek are sought in part because we have the means to seek them, and how we conceive of those ends is itself influenced by the technology which we have available to us to realize them. If Matthews is right, for a long time the concept of health was conceived as something to be obtained within natural boundaries; with the advent of scientific medicine, it becomes something which transcends them.

The constitution of the problematic

The upshot of all this is that, except in a few restricted cases perhaps, technology should not be regarded as the handmaiden of human needs and desires, but a highly important contributor to their formation. Consider now the second presupposition – that a technical problem is constituted by what we already find problematic. In many instances, it is true, technological progress consists in finding better ways of accomplishing given tasks. Nevertheless, such improvements, even when accurately described as increases in efficiency, may be *revealed by* and not merely *embodied in* the technology. For example, it seems plausible to think that the most immediately perceived benefit of keyhole surgery was its ability to accomplish more efficiently the precise tasks which the more invasive surgery of older methods also attempted. But keyhole surgery has also been found to speed the healing process by requiring far shorter periods of hospitalization, a result partly of psychological as well as physiological factors. The original aim, let us say, was to spill less blood, but the final outcome is considerably better than this from the point of view of successful treatment. There is no good reason to suppose that we could have anticipated this in advance of adopting the new technology, and this is why it is right to say that the improved benefits were revealed by and not merely embodied in the new technique.

The truth of this observation might be thought less consequential than initially appears. Is it not the case that effective and speedier recovery from illness was what was sought throughout? This is a query related to the earlier discussion of generalized needs. The point is that we can allow that new techniques *reveal* a greater improvement than was at first anticipated, and on a wider front, while at the same time continuing to hold that their value resides in their increased ability to address what was regarded as problematic all along, in this case illness. Now in the particular example of keyhole surgery, this may be so. I shall not argue the case. It is much less clear that the same point could be made about every possible example.

It is not even generally true of medicine. Medical technology, in fact, seems to me replete with examples of innovations that alter the parameters of the problematic. Before the invention of life-support machines, for instance, the question of whether a persistent vegetative state (PVS) is tantamount to death was not a problem. Anyone who was in such a state would in a very short time be dead in the normal way. What the new technology revealed was a gap between life at a purely biological level and life at a conscious level, for with the assistance of technology the former could continue when the latter was at an end. Is this life or death? And what do we do about it? Here we have a new problem, it seems, something which was not problematic before.

An objector might persist; there is still an underlying continuity, the concern with preserving life and preventing death. But this is just the point. Is the preservation of someone in a persistent vegetative state the preservation of life *in the relevant sense*? We think life worth preserving because life is valuable. What this new technology did was to put in our hands the possibility of sustaining 'life' whose character is such that its value is questionable, and precisely because this is so, the obligation to preserve life in the form of PVS is much less clear than it was. Before, we knew what the duty to preserve life implied; now we do not.

In short, technology may start out as a new means to an old end, but its development turns out to have serious implications for our conception of the end itself. This will come as a surprise only if we are inclined to the third presupposition built into Postman's 'test' – that technology is *essentially* purposeful.

Means and ends

From a philosophical point of view this third assumption is the most interesting of the three I have identified. Postman's test applies only if technology is exclusively purposive, that is, *entirely* a matter of means to ends. It is an assumption which it is easy to make, and made easier yet by its having this further advantage: it provides us with a conceptually simple standard of assessment, namely usefulness. The first point to be made against it, however, arises from just this feature. In the accomplishment of human purposes there is the possibility of more than efficiency; there is also the matter of style. Take for example satisfying the desire to eat. If this were just a matter of supplying the needs of nutrition ever more efficiently we could not explain an important aspect of food preparation – taste. One recipe may be as good as another from the point of view of digestibility, safety to health and nutritional value, and yet be preferable because of its taste and appearance. Moreover, improvement in taste and appearance is most often a matter of discovery. I can discover, *ab initio* so to speak, how delicious the mixture of two flavours is, having had neither a pre-existent desire to find a new combination nor even a belief that such was waiting to be found. In a similar way I can discover the advantages of a different method of cooking. Such is (one) theme of Charles Lamb's famous story about the discovery of roast pork. The technology of the kitchen can in this way be a matter of pure experimentation.

So too with other tasks. Computer graphics now allows many more people than ever before to experiment with presentation. They already know, let us suppose, what it is they want to say, but they discover, by experimentation, more interesting and arresting ways of saying it. The attraction of this new technology is not simply, or even mainly, an increase in speed and a reduction in cost over pen and paint, but in stylistic and expressive possibilities.

Ignoring the importance of style is not the main fault in the assumption of essential purposiveness, however. A more fundamental error is the implicit supposition that the distinction between 'end' and 'means' is categorial rather than relative. The difference between the categorial and the relative is most easily illustrated by judgements of size. 'Large' and 'small' can be thought of as contraries. A thing cannot be *both* large *and* small, it is easily assumed. But this is false. A large mouse can be a small animal; a large raspberry can be a small fruit. 'Large' and 'small' are essentially relative judgements, which is to say, they are judgements relative to the sorts of things they qualify. So too, with ends and means. These are relative judgements. Something can be a means relative to one thing and an end relative to another. My taking a job in a factory may be the means to the end of earning the fees for a course; the fees earned are the means by which I pay for the course, which in turn may be the means to gaining an engineering degree, my gaining a degree the means to the end of securing a career in electronics, and so on. In this example (and the examples can be multiplied indefinitely, of course) each stage is *both* means *and* end, depending on the perspective from which it is viewed.

What is the importance of this observation? Its significance is that we cannot rest content with usefulness on its own as a measure of benefit. A means is useful to an end, but if 'means' is a relative term, then so too is 'useful'. Were we restricted to the useful, our estimate of benefit would in an important way be incomplete. In fact, so incomplete would it be that we could attribute no real significance at all to instrumental effectiveness, which, considered by itself, is worthless. This is a point made by J.L. Stocks in a once famous essay entitled 'The Limits to Purpose'.

So far as you are wholly concentrated on bringing about a certain result, clearly the quicker and easier it is brought about the better. Your resolve to secure a sufficiency of food for yourself and your family will induce you to spend weary days in tilling the ground and tending livestock; but if Nature provided food and meat in abundance ready for the table, you would thank Nature for sparing you much labour and consider yourself so much the better off. An executed purpose, in short, is a transaction in which the time and energy spent on the execution are balanced against the resulting assets, and the ideal case is one in which the former approximates to zero and the latter to infinity. Purpose, then, justifies the efforts it exacts only conditionally, by their fruits.

(Stocks, p. 20)

Stocks' point can be applied directly to technology. In so far as the benefit of technology arises from its usefulness, it loses its value when something better takes its place, and if we pursue this line of thought the ideal world would be one in which technology is of no benefit at all, because we do not need to use it. To regard technology as essentially purposeful, then, is to make the mistake of supposing that usefulness is valuable in and for itself. It is not; 'the useful' is of consequence only in so far as it is serves something else. Assessing real benefits, certainly, requires us to pursue a chain of means to ends, but this chain of assessment only produces an answer if, somewhere, it comes to an end. Where is the end to be found? The answer is that we must assess the advantages of technological innovation in terms of the *value* of the ends to which it is a useful means.

To summarize. It is tempting to think, as Postman's question implies and Berry's test asserts, that the evaluative assessment of technological innovation is a matter of deciding whether the ends we already have are better achieved by the new means with which we are presented. By this account of the matter, technological innovation (however ingenious) will be redundant if it does not solve the problems or further the ends of which we are and perhaps always have been possessed, ends set for us by recurrent, generalizable desires. Against this we can now say, first, that technological innovation is, in the ways I have suggested, at least in part a process of experiment and discovery; second, that it both enlarges existing ends and alters our conception of them; third, that this makes it a process of development which can throw up wholly new aims and purposes. It follows that the business of assessing the value of any new technology is more complex than the simple means-to-end model suggests. When we add the fourth and further point that means and ends are not categorially distinct but only relatively so, an implication of considerable significance emerges: it is a mistake to think that the assessment of technology can rest content with the idea of usefulness; it necessarily passes on to the idea of the valuable.

Cost–benefit analysis

This summary casts additional light on a familiar idea alluded to earlier – that technological innovation can readily be assessed in terms of costs and benefits. The basic idea of cost–benefit analysis is very straightforward. If benefits outweigh costs, then we are net gainers and ought to adopt the new technology; when they do not, we are losers and ought not to do so. Cost–benefit analysis is attractively simple, but in order to make assessments in this way we need to be clear about the basis of cost and the basis of benefit. In most cases this is harder to do than might at first be imagined. For one thing, the associated costs can be imponderable. A dramatic innovation like the Internet has very many and very widespread consequences. These are extremely difficult to predict and hence to assess. We know that the amount of money spent on computers has been vast, though it is hard to say just how much it is. Indeed Janet Hyland, a network strategy consultant, believes that 'no one will ever know how expensive it is' (quoted in Tenner, p. 199). Both local and international networking have had very many effects, but just what these are is difficult to itemize with any degree of precision. Part of the difficulty is determining the timescale over which the assessment is to be made. But even where we are able to draw a line around the chain of effects in both temporal and geographical extension, the problems may be no less intractable. In practice, the sums both of costs and benefits are often incalculable.

This is an important fact which should at the least temper our enthusiasm for the cost–benefit approach. Much more important from a philosophical point of view is a conceptual rather than a factual question: what is to count as a benefit? The strategy of cost–benefit analysis presupposes both estimability and commensurability in input and outcome. That is to say, it supposes *both* that we can estimate the costs and benefits *and* that there is some common medium in terms of which they can be compared. A relatively simple illustration of cost–benefit analysis would be advertising. Is the monetary cost of additional advertising outweighed by the additional monetary value of sales? In this particular case the requirements of estimability and commensurability seem easy to satisfy, though even here less obviously quantifiable effects on 'image' may come into play. Still, a company can know how much it has spent on advertising and how much has come in sales, and both quantities can be cast in monetary terms. The simplicity of this case is comparatively rare, however. Consider, by way of contrast, the comparison we might try to make between two holidays. We can tell easily enough how much each costs; but how should we estimate the benefits and can they be compared by means of the commensurable medium of money? This is much less obvious. How is the benefit of sea and sun to be compared with the interest in visiting historic places? Even if I know that I enjoyed one holiday much more than I did the other, I may still be quite unable to put a *monetary* value of the higher level of enjoyment and thus unable to compare its additional benefit with its relative cost.

The example of sales and advertising, in effect, invokes the idea of usefulness: has the new advertising medium been more instrumentally *useful* in producing the same end, namely increased sales? The second example, on the other hand, introduces a different sort of scale: was the second holiday of greater *value* than the former? What this shows is that cost–benefit analysis, however alluring its simplicity, cannot adequately deal with the difference between the useful and the valuable, a difference that we have seen other reason to highlight. It is this distinction, not that between cost and benefit, which we most need to understand.

The useful and the valuable

The distinction between the useful and the valuable is of great philosophical importance and requires further explanation. One way of explaining it is this. The activities of any individual can be divided into two broad categories – work and leisure. There are other distinctions with which this can be (but ought not to be) confused. The distinction between work and leisure is not that between the dreary and the pleasurable, for instance. Some people find their work a source of great personal satisfaction and others find that leisure activities can pall. Nor is it a distinction between employment and non-employment. The possessor of vast inherited wealth, who is not employed, is working, in the relevant sense, when he keeps track of his millions or draws more money from the bank. Similarly, unemployed people in receipt of social security are working, in this same sense, when they stand in line to collect their welfare benefit or fill in the forms bureaucracy requires. The distinction between work and leisure, then, is really between those activities which are necessary to live, and those which make living worthwhile.

We can express this distinction as one between useful activities (work) and valuable activities (leisure). Of course, in the life of one individual any given activity may be simultaneously useful and valuable (this is perhaps the mark of a 'profession' or 'vocation' as opposed to a mere 'job'), but there must always be some such distinction in every assessment of worth just because we can always ask of any activity (or object) that is useful – what is it useful *for*? And because we can always ask this question, we need some further evaluative conception which will answer it and which is not itself open to the very same question, otherwise we are launched on a regress, a way of trying to estimate benefit that is necessarily incomplete. This further conception, which brings the business of estimation to completion, is what we may call 'the valuable'. In short, while every human life will contain actions and objects whose purpose is to sustain life (the useful), it must also contain others whose purpose is to make life worth sustaining (the valuable).

The usefulness of the useful is, in a way, easy to assess, because it lies exclusively in causal efficiency: does a means that purports to be better actually bring about the desired end in the quickest and most cost-effective way? If it does, then it is useful. But what of the value of the valuable? What determines this? There is an answer implicit in the expression 'the desired end' which we have been using: namely, that value lies in the satisfaction of desires. This explanation of value in terms of the satisfaction of desire has a long, if not entirely venerable, philosophical history. Its most famous exponent is David Hume, and to examine it we need to return to his memorable dictum quoted earlier: 'Reason is and only ought to be the slave of the passions'.

The implications of this dictum can be easily brought out by an example drawn from recent technology. Computers have made possible the itemizing of telephone bills. Before this was a possibility, let us agree, no one felt its absence. Now that itemizing *is* possible, people can and do desire it, and hence tend to prefer telephone systems that permit it over those that do not. To conclude that itemized bills represent an increase in *value*, however, that in some way or other they enrich our lives (albeit modestly), we must ask where precisely the additional value lies. Is it in satisfying a desire? The claim that it is carries a curious implication – namely, that human beings are the playthings and not the masters of technological innovation. That is to say, they are *subject* to the dictate of desires which are neither of their own choosing or under their direction. So, in the example of itemized bills the picture is one in which we are simply presented with this new invention and either do or do not find awakened in us a desire for it. If we do, then it is valuable; if we do not, it is not. What the picture rules out is any mediation by the reflective intelligence, any raising of the question: 'Is this new invention *worth* desiring?'

This is not a very welcome implication, yet it is a necessary corollary of the dictum that reason is and only ought to be the slave of the passions. To reject it therefore, suggests that we should reject (or at least seriously question) Hume's dictum and deny that the basis of the valuable (as opposed to the useful) is adequately explained by the satisfaction of desire.

So strong is the grip of Humeanism in contemporary thinking about these issues, however, that it often seems very difficult to say where else it might lie. In *The Road Ahead* Bill Gates remarks that there is never a reliable map for unexplored territory. But is the information highway really unexplored territory? It is fairly easy to state the advantages that it has over telephone, fax, letters or libraries. Most of these have to do with access, speed, storage and so on. But if this is all that there were to be said, the Internet would not constitute a new source of value, merely a useful new way of doing things whose value is already established. What new possibilities does the Internet introduce and how, if they truly are new benefits, is their value to be assessed? The crucial problem here, as I remarked in the introduction, is not to *anticipate* these new possibilities, which is what Gates is trying to do, but to put in place some conceptual framework in terms of which their innovatory character can be evaluated. And the important point is that we want a way of thinking about the source of value underlying this assessment which does not make passive victims of technology's users and consumers.

So, something more needs to be said about the satisfaction of desire. There is an old contrast of considerable significance which is relevant at this point. Hume's contention is that things are valuable because we desire them. An alternative contention is that it is rational to desire things if and only if they are valuable. To believe the first is to subscribe to a *subjective* explanation of value – the valuable is *constituted* by our desires; to believe the second is to subscribe to an *objective* explanation of value – the rationally desirable must be based on the truly valuable.

My own inclination is to the objective interpretation. This is because it seems obvious that people can genuinely desire harmful and worthless things, and the fact that they do have such desires does not in itself seem to bestow any value. In other words, desiring the harmful or the trivial does not make it any less harmful or trivial. For example, addicts unquestionably want drugs; this does not make them good for them. The collector of bus tickets wants bus tickets; this *in itself* lends them no intrinsic interest. What this implies is that, *contra* Hume, the psychological state of desiring can *track* the desirable (in the objective sense) or it can fail to do so.

Suppose this alternative to Hume is true. What then is the mark of the objectively desirable, the truly worthwhile? One possible answer can be generated by returning to a way of thinking that has been unfashionable for most of this century – the appeal to progress. Few deny (who could?) that technological advances in recent times have been more striking and have had more widespread effects than those of possibly any preceding century. Mere technological advance is not a sufficient guarantee of betterment in a larger sense, however. Is the Armalite rifle, for instance, a progression on the bow and arrow? The reason we might hesitate over saying that it is, though it accomplishes the same purpose – the killing of enemies – with far greater efficiency, lies in the thought that we would be even better off without the need for either. Killing is bad and better ways of killing, though they are instrumentally better, do not make killing itself any better. It is not necessary to enter into a proper discussion of the many issues this remark raises to make the point I want to make. We can approach the assessment of weaponry in a narrower or a larger framework. Within the narrower one of efficacy there has been progress. Within the larger one of international relations and human welfare this is much less clear. Yet the wider framework is obviously relevant to an adequate assessment of this important branch of modern technology. The construction of this wider framework is a major philosophical task: to delineate the features of an evaluatively more praiseworthy world order. (The reader will find the subject addressed at length in my book *The Shape of the Past*, which is listed in the bibliography.) Obviously more needs to be said about this, but for the moment it is sufficient to state the thought I have in mind at its most abstract. Better weaponry is better instrumentally. But it is 'better' *tout court* only in so far as it forms part of a better world. So too with the Internet. The improvements it promises are improvements in so far as they make for a better world.

Thus stated such a contention sounds vacuous, platitudinous even, unless we answer some all-important questions: better in what respect? And who is to say? Nonetheless, despite its abstraction, such a conclusion has interesting and important implications. Faust, it will be recalled, at least in some versions of the myth, obtained unlimited wealth and power in exchange for his soul. We may interpret this as meaning that he was required to abandon any claim to a wider judgement on the ultimate value of things. Faust was confined to the accomplishment of strictly mundane desires: you want power and success, and for a price you can have it. But do not ask about the true value of those desires. Assessing the Faustian bargain properly, therefore, requires us to occupy a point of view other than that of our current, felt desires. This point of view is that of a wide cultural and moral frame. In this respect the myth of Faust is to be contrasted with the Promethean myth. Again, this comes in different versions, but in *Prometheus Bound* he is represented as the inspirer of both technology and the quest for knowledge, the Titan who restored fire to human beings, in defiance of Zeus. The mastery of nature which Prometheus represents, unlike that of Faust, does not confine itself to the accomplishment of human desire, but continually strives for a larger understanding such as the gods might jealously guard as peculiarly their own. Achieving this point of view is a very large task and its sheer size makes it daunting, which is why Prometheus, in later nineteenth-century versions, is an icon of Romantic heroism. But the difficulty of the task should not make us think of it as impossible; indeed it is not so difficult to make some headway with it.

Moral freedom and political neutrality

Chief among the difficulties that explicating and defending an objective conception of what is and is not valuable faces is the resistance that arises from the rejection of moral absolutism and fear of political totalitarianism, a resistance characteristic of the West in the twentieth century. In most previous ages there were, and in other contemporary places there are, believers in absolute right and wrong. Such people are prepared, on the one hand to kill and oppress in defence of these absolutes, and on the other to die for them as martyrs and heroes. It is arguable, though far from demonstrable, that this sort of absolutism was the source of the ferocious religious wars in Europe, wars which the founding intention of the United States was designed to overcome (historically an even more questionable contention in my view). Whatever the truth of this, there can be little doubt that modern political thinking has been profoundly influenced by the idea of toleration. As a consequence, the dominant political philosophy of the contemporary period – liberal democratic theory – has striven to base itself on fundamental values that enjoy a certain sort of neutrality.

The claims for this neutrality rest on two important contentions. First, there is the belief that killing and persecuting for the sake of some supposedly 'higher' moral or religious end is indefensible. Let us agree that it is. It is crucial to observe however that, if so, our agreement rests upon an assumption which necessarily presupposes, and hence does not deny, an objective conception of value. It supposes, in fact, that killing or persecuting in the name of culture-bound religious or moral codes violates yet more important values – the lives, freedom and welfare of other human beings. This may be true; for my own part I have no inclination to dispute it. True or not, however, it invokes a set of values no less objective than those it seeks to displace: to kill others because of their religion is wrong – not wrong 'relatively speaking', but wrong *simpliciter*.

Simpliciter is not the same as 'absolutely', however. Absolute values I take to be values without qualification or exception, values which are not commensurable and can never be compromised. Now it is perfectly consistent to hold that there are no such exceptionless values, that is to say, no values that can never be traded off against others according to contingent circumstances, while at the same time interpreting trade-offs of this kind as trade-offs between the objectively valid. Indeed, it is difficult to interpret that in any other way, because the need for a trade-off *implies* a value independent of choice and desire. This is true even of benefits of a strictly personal kind. I may settle for a trade-off between, for instance, the excitement of hang-gliding and the risks to physical injury it poses without this calling into question the objective good of the excitement and the objective good of avoiding injury. It is only this, in fact, that makes sense of the idea of 'getting the balance right'. It follows that though they are commonly compounded, objectivity and absolutism are not the same.

The second basis of the modern conception of neutrality lies, as I have already noted, in a strong belief in the value of toleration. Once again, however, stressing the importance of toleration does not militate against an objective conception of value. On the contrary, it presupposes it. Subjectivism about values and toleration of social differences are often thought to go hand in hand, but properly speaking, I am only called upon to tolerate things which I believe to be truly wrong or bad. I have no need of tolerance with respect to *mere* differences – of taste, for example. I am not called upon to 'tolerate' your choice from the restaurant menu simply because it differs from mine. It is only if and when I believe that someone else's freely chosen decision is not merely different but *wrong* that I am called upon to respect their freedom by tolerating their erroneous beliefs and misguided actions. Toleration, then, is a concomitant not of relativism or subjectivism, but of a commitment to the objective value of freedom.

If this is right, there are values (freedom being one) which transcend felt desire. Toleration implies the suppression of a desire to stop or hinder others in the name of a higher value which is not itself, therefore, a felt desire. Such a conclusion supports both the rejection of the Humean dictum and the contention that we must locate the benefits of innovatory instrumental means in the permanent pantheon of transcendental values. 'Transcendental' here does not mean 'other-worldly' (though a case can be made for thinking that the ultimate source of value must lie beyond the realms of ordinary human experience) but Promethean in the sense explained previously. For present purposes it need only be taken to mean values that are necessarily abiding for all forms of human communication and interrelation, and hence rise above and regulate the desires we find ourselves having.

From the point of view of avoiding strife this is a welcome conclusion. Despite common opinion to the contrary, to conceive of values as ultimately rooted in felt desire is not to make room for respectful negotiation and compromise, but to imply that at bottom there can *only* be conflict – my desires against yours. By contrast, if there are objective values we can hope, mutually, to discover what they are and thus *resolve* our disagreements. This is a possibility which many find unpersuasive because it leaves unanswered this most important question: how are we to tell, and who is to say, what these values are?

There is a long-standing tradition in moral and political philosophy – one which the 'neutralist' political philosophy dominant in the second half of this century has tended to embrace – that offers an answer to this question. It goes by the general name of 'contractualism'. The idea behind it is that the ultimate values which must govern social and moral relations are those which would be agreed upon by rational agents stripped, as it were, of their personal preferences and particular interests. This is the conception at work in the writings of the century's most influential political philosopher – John Rawls. In a sequence of books and essays Rawls has elaborated at great length the thesis that the values which should structure the fundamental constitution of social and political life are those which can be found to comprise what he calls an 'overlapping consensus' between groups of individuals who in many other respects are divided by deep differences.

The amount that has been written about Rawls' conception of social morality is vast, and there is neither point in nor scope for considering it in detail here. It is sufficient for present purposes to draw attention to one element in the Rawlsian strategy. This is the uncovering of the overlapping consensus by an exchange between competing points of view. One difficulty with the realization of this strategy is that it remains unclear in Rawls whether the exchange is one between hypothetical deliberators or real ones. If it is the first, there is a question about how such *hypothetical* deliberation can uncover *actual* consensus. If it is the second, if it is *actual* consensus that matters, there is the obvious objection that real political deliberation does not take place in the pages of a philosophy book, but must actually take place in the public forum. The most that philosophy can show is what people ought to agree to; it cannot show that they have so agreed.

Political theory of a normative kind, then, must at some point give way to political practice; this fact turns our attention to the realities of the democratic process. Does the democratic process realize, at least in part, the sort of deliberation out of which real consensus can arise? The best we can say, to date, is that it does so in a very imperfect form. We know that in even the best-ordered societies the democratic process is not in fact one in which every opinion has free and equal opportunity of expression. Moreover, in practice democracy is a system where wealth and power can be used to affect, and on occasions effect, electoral outcomes.

It is on the strength of this background belief about consensus and democracy that one of the most important and ambitious claims about the Internet has been made. It has been argued, for instance, that the public and interactive nature of the Internet presents us with the means by which, for the first time, true democracy (and hence real consensus) is possible. Is this correct, and if it is, is it to be welcomed? These are two of the questions to be addressed in the next chapter. To appreciate their significance for the theme of this chapter, however, a summary of the argument up to this point will be useful.

We began with the question: how are we to assess the value of technological innovation in advance of knowing exactly where it might lead? The initial suggestion considered was that we should ask what problem or problems such innovation can be expected to solve. Upon examination, however, it emerged that this very natural question is importantly limited. It supposes that the problems we seek to solve are independent of the means available for solving them. This, we have seen, is false. Postman's 'test question' further supposes that 'the problematic' is constituted subjectively, by what is felt to be a problem. This too is false. But more importantly yet, it implies that the significance of technology is a matter of instrumentality – usefulness. Further reflection and analysis shows, to the contrary, that 'usefulness' is an essentially incomplete conception of worth, and that it requires a further reference to values which are the final ends which mere usefulness serves and in terms of which it has to be shown to constitute a real benefit. Such values, though often construed as arising directly from human desires, are better interpreted objectively – which is to say, interpreted as standing above and shaping the more immediate ends of felt desire. The discovery and realization of these values creates an essential, and a larger, context – the context of a better world to which truly useful technology is a better means.

What are these values? One answer to this question which has been canvassed extensively in contemporary moral and political philosophy (as well as in social thinking more broadly) is that they are the values which will command agreement or consensus after a process of widespread social deliberation and debate. Such deliberation brings into dialogue the many different voices that go to make up the pluralist societies of the modern world, a dialogue which serves both to uncover common ground and to forge a common agenda. How is this deliberation to be contrived? Another answer to this further question is equally familiar: it is to be effected through the democratic process. This is one explanation of the rise and (apparently) universal aspiration to democratic social and political forms. However, up to the present, democratic institutions have functioned only imperfectly and have been subject to the distorting influences of unequal distributions of wealth and power. Could it be the case that the technological innovation of the Internet might significantly alter this? If so, we have (by a somewhat circuitous route) arrived at an answer to the topic of this chapter which can be made to apply to the technology of the Internet. Technology is truly valuable if it raises the prospect of a better world. A more democratic world would be a better one. Now, for the first time, we have the means – the Internet – to effect this improvement.

The cogency of these last two claims – that a more democratic world is a better world and that the Internet can bring this about – provides the starting point of the next chapter.

4 The Internet as democracy

Although the use and popularity of the Internet is advancing with unprecedented speed, we are still only on the very edge of its development. Among the dreams that might be entertained for it, and are actively entertained in some quarters, is that of a world of far greater freedom of expression and democratic control than anything which human history has yet contrived. Whatever the plausibility of this speculation from a technical point of view, the *desirability* of the dream turns importantly on two questions with which we can make some headway in advance of knowing precisely what the future holds. Is democracy a good thing, and does what we know about the Internet give us good reason to think that this is the way to realize it? So powerful are the democratic presuppositions of the present age that it is difficult to persuade people to take the first of these questions seriously and approach it in a genuine spirit of critical inquiry. For this reason, though it is of the greatest importance for present purposes to address some fundamental questions in the theory of democracy, I shall begin with the second issue – the democratic nature of the Internet.

Direct versus representative democracy

What is it about the Internet that has led to the idea that it might be a powerful democratic instrument? The word 'forum' nowadays has largely metaphorical meaning. Its etymological roots, however, lie in the Latin word for 'market place', a physical location where Roman citizens gathered to discuss matters of public concern.

Ancient Rome was not a democracy, but the existence of a literal political 'forum' can just as readily be applied to those ancient Greek city states which were. In them, Athens most famously of course, citizens also gathered in one place and took part equally and collectively, not merely in debate and discussion, but in decision-making. Athenian democracy has been romanticized, for (as has often been noted) this form of democracy was only made possible by the fact that these were small self-governing cities, and in reality, even in them, a large proportion of the population – women and slaves notably – were excluded from the process. In the context of much larger states, and with the advent of near universal suffrage, the literal notion of a political forum has to be abandoned, which is why, for the most part, we use the expression metaphorically nowadays. To put it at its plainest, in the modern state there is nowhere big enough for even relatively small electorates to gather.

An expanded voting public, therefore, necessitates an important qualification of what might be thought to be the ancient democratic ideal. Today, and for a very long time, a democratic system of government, to be realistic, must be representative. The most celebrated early example of representative democracy is the Icelandic *Althing*, established in AD 930. It consisted, not in a popular assembly, but in a gathering of forty-eight chieftains who spoke and voted on behalf of the groups they represented. No doubt this was an arrangement which did preserve a fairly close relationship between the formulation of laws and the people to whom these laws applied (for one thing, the chieftains were accompanied by supporters), but even this model is impracticable for all but very small societies. The expansion of population inevitably entails a circumstance in which the vast majority of citizens are excluded from the literal decision-making forum. As a consequence, the only part they can play in the process is that of providing and choosing those who will represent them there. And this is how it is in the modern world.

The contrast between direct and representative democracy and what that means for the democratic ideal has been the subject of an enormous amount of discussion. Are representatives to be regarded as mere delegates, whose duty is to vote in accordance with the wishes of those who elected them? Or are they to be accorded the status of representatives more properly so-called, who, though they must be mindful of the interests of their constitutents, are expected to make their own decisions on the political questions of the day? If we follow the first line of thought, practical difficulties rapidly arise. First, in any real constituency there will be differences of opinion on specific issues between those who, nonetheless, voted for the same representative. Even in the rare case of a single-issue candidate, where it is clear which way the person elected should vote, the conception of delegate effectively excludes those in the electorate who voted on the other side from any further part in the debate. Second, political business cannot in any case always be anticipated in advance. What is the delegate to do with respect to political issues which arise after the election? Given that political life is heavily subject to unpredicted and unpredictable events, the conception of elected representative as delegate either leaves decision-makers paralysed (since they lack instructions from their electors) or it puts very many political issues out of the reach of the electorate.

Such considerations have inclined most democratic theorists to prefer the conception of elected representatives as autonomous political deliberators who are not so much mandated by those they represent, as charged with the responsibility of conducting political affairs on their behalf. This second conception, however, has problems of its own. If representatives are free to decide for themselves on what the best action or policy is, there is clearly the ever-present possibility that they depart from the wishes and preferences of their electorates, not the preferences they had on issues current at the time of the election, but their wishes with respect to issues that have newly arisen. In this case, though something of the democratic ideal may be said to remain – government for the people – a more important part falls into abeyance, namely government *by* the people.

The general upshot of these considerations would thus appear to be this: practical realities require us to accept the necessity of representative rather than direct democracy. Once we do so however, we face an unattractive dilemma. Either we treat elected representatives as mere ciphers who cast their votes without any thought of their own (the p͟.   ͟ch representatives to the electoral college that chooses   ͟merican President find themselves) and who are politically paralysed in the face of new eventualities or we must empower them in a way that effectively transfers power from the people to the people's representatives.

There are of course refinements and responses that can be made to and on behalf of both conceptions, though I do not myself think that these make much difference to the fundamental problem. More effectively, in support of either it can be said that the dilemma only arises because the position of ordinary citizens in a democracy has been described too narrowly. It takes the fact that voters cannot participate in parliamentary or congressional debates to imply that between elections voters are wholly excluded from the political process. This is obviously false, at least in a reasonably free society. Through the press and television, political rallies and direct contact with representatives, voters have both the means and the opportunity to feed their beliefs and preferences into the deliberations of those they have elected, whether regarded as delegates or representatives in the fuller sense. The voice of the people need not, and does not, fall silent between elections. Nor is this merely a matter of the people at large expressing a view. It is evident that in working democracies views expressed between elections have an influence on the deliberations, and on the votes, of legislators. In other words, the claim that the participation of ordinary citizens in a representative democracy is limited to election time is false to actual experience. Government *by* the people can continue, in part, between elections.

Now it is worth observing that while these are important facts about contemporary politics, they are the outcome of historical achievements. One of the classic discussions of the delegate versus representative debate is Edmund Burke's famous *Letter to the Electors of Bristol* (1785). At the time at which Burke was writing, the conditions of political life, and hence the conditions of democracy, were importantly different to those which prevail now. Then, in the absence of telephone and television, motor transport, railways and aeroplanes, daily newspapers and all the other forms of communication which the modern world takes for granted, it was much nearer the truth to say that electors had an important role at election times, but thereafter could bring little influence to bear on the course of political life. Indeed, the era of Burke, though separated from Magna Carta and the origins of Parliament by a longer period of time than it is from ours, was closer in its political circumstances, precisely because of technological differences. Members of early Parliaments, which only met for sessions of limited lengths, were neither subject to nor had opportunities for consultation with the opinions of those who had elected them. This was a condition that also applied at the founding of the state with the first self-consciously democratic constitution – the United States of America. Exchange of opinion between the first Congressmen and Senators and the scattered citizenry of the former colonies they represented was seriously restricted, not least by the sheer size of the new country.

New means of communication and new avenues for the expression of political opinion greatly altered this, and these new means were owed entirely to technological innovation, beginning with the printing press. What they did, it can be argued, was to supply a deficiency in representative democracy, and thus bring it closer to the original ideal. These observations, both about democracy and technology, set the scene and provide a promising basis for claims about the Internet. If the availability and efficiency of the means of communication and expression are important elements in the realization of democracy, and if in the Internet we have an unprecedentedly good means of communication and expression, we may infer that the Internet puts within our grasp an unprecedentedly good form of democracy.

The advantages of e-mail and the power of the web page

This important and interesting suggestion warrants close examination because, whatever criticisms may eventually be brought against it, initially it can be strengthened considerably by noting some of the real advantages of the Internet over other forms of communication. Consider first e-mail. E-mail is attractive to many users because it combines the benefits of telephone, letter and fax, without many of the corresponding disadvantages. For example, an e-mail can serve in exactly the same way as a letter, but minus the necessity of finding a stamp and a postbox. No doubt this is why increasing numbers of people are e-mailing newspapers, radio and television. Hitherto, mild but nonetheless important preconditions like buying or having stamps, paper and envelopes acted as deterrents. Now, sitting at my desk, and with an idle moment or two perhaps, it is easier by far to fill it by expressing my opinion in the public forum of radio or the press than it was only a short time ago.

E-mail also has the immediacy of the telephone. I can communicate with any part of the world far more rapidly than a letter would take, as rapidly as I can by telephone in fact. But there are advantages over the telephone also. For one thing, there is much less exposure of a personal kind, and as a result what I say by e-mail, despite its speed and immediacy, can be considered. I *can* respond very rapidly, but unlike the telephone I am not *obliged* to do so and I do not need to think on my feet. By the same token, the person I am calling is not forced into an unconsidered response either. Moreover, both of us can write and respond in a very limited way, more limited, I think, than is ever the practice for telephone, letter or fax. It is common, for example, for people to send one-line replies or queries, because it is easy and cheap to do so. Very rarely do people pick up the phone, dial across the world, utter a single sentence and put it down again. Still less will they go to the trouble of writing and posting a letter in order to do this.

The immediacy of the telephone has disadvantages over and above the pressure it creates to make unconsidered responses, and these are disadvantages that e-mail also avoids. If I want to communicate with you by telephone, you must be at a specific place at a specific time, that is, at the end of the line when I call. Otherwise, no communication takes place. Even if I do, then, without a complicated and probably secretive taping system, there is no record of what was said between us. A letter, by contrast, though slower and less immediate, can be read at the convenience of the recipient and can be retained for future reference. In these respects, e-mail combines the immediacy of the telephone with the advantages of a letter: if you are there at the time, you can respond; if not, my message awaits you, and you can print it off for the purposes of your files, as I can with your response.

A further important point to be observed is that these advantages are not just advantages to individuals, but to groups. The ease, cheapness and convenience with which individuals may communicate with each other by e-mail applies to communication between sets of people, and hence implies far greater ease of group organization and management. It is, for instance, far simpler and (at present) very considerably less expensive to circulate a message (notice of a meeting, say) to large numbers of interested people than it is to telephone or write them all a letter. Now while there are many personal, educational and commercial benefits to be derived from these advantages for group communication, they are politically significant also, which is what concerns us in this chapter. The formation and maintenance of political parties, lobbies and interest groups is an important way of filling the gap between the ideal of direct democracy and the necessity of representative democracy. If this is more or less easily done, depending upon the technology available to citizens, we can attribute greater democratic benefits to different forms of technology, in this case electronic mail.

With the advent of e-mail, then, the contribution of both individuals and groups to public debate can now be made at much less expense and inconvenience than hitherto, and without the risk of personal exposure that deters many from any form of political participation. It would be surprising indeed if these advantages were not capitalized on by political agencies and there is good evidence that this is already well under way. This is good for democracy, according to the analysis I have presented, and therefore good full stop, *if* greater democracy is something to be welcomed, a question we have yet to examine. There is, of course, another side to it and much more to be said about the impact on group formation in particular. This is a subject which will be discussed further in a later chapter. For the moment, however, we can record that there is reason to regard the advantage of e-mail over previous forms of communication as a significant point in favour of those who regard the Internet as an important element in democratic advance.

E-mail, of course, is only one aspect of the Internet, and a limited one in many respects. But other features can plausibly be construed as having democratic advantages also. Take, for instance, the construction of web pages. Web pages can be thought of as the catalogues or showcases of companies, institutions, organizations and individuals. They are more impressive and versatile than even the glossiest catalogue, however, since they can contain sound and moving pictures, as well as text and illustration, and can provide opportunities for response and interaction.

A web page is a body of electronic impulses, or digital information, stored in a machine somewhere, a 'server' that has a specific physical location. However, thanks to the technology of hyperlinks, this digital information may be accessed from anywhere in the world and (given suitable software) the business of accessing it constructs the pictures, text, sound and so on, that the constructor has provided, on the computer screen of the accessor. In fact, as far as users are concerned the language and technology of digital information and servers can be forgotten or ignored. We need to know nothing of these things to make, access and interact with text and images. Moreover, our ability to do so is virtually unlimited in space and time. Anyone anywhere at anytime, even with relatively limited means, can put things on and take things off the web. More importantly, in a way, as greater and greater amounts of software become available, both for purchase from commercial providers and freely donated by enthusiasts, the ordinary citizen can deploy impressive forms of presentation while lacking the skills, not just of engineers, but of artists, typographers and experts.

To appreciate this, compare the Internet with radio and television. Even in these days of indefinitely many radio and television channels, and dramatically reduced costs of basic broadcasting, the possibility of individuals and small groups assembling the resources and know-how to put themselves or their views on air is still severely restricted, so restricted in fact that it is a practical impossiblity for most. By contrast, individuals and groups with limited time, resources and skills can avail themselves of the technology of the Internet and, literally, present themselves and their message to the world. Once again, there are great personal and commercial benefits to be derived from this and it may be that it is chiefly benefits of this sort which are the principal driving force behind the Internet's spread and development; but there are political benefits also, benefits which can easily be interpreted as filling up the democratic deficit, that is, filling the gap between representative and direct democracy.

It might be replied that the advantages of this new technology have been considerably overstated. Let us agree that, relatively speaking, the Internet with both e-mail and web pages extends technical means of communication and expression to a far wider number of people than hitherto. Even so, it requires (at a minimum) the high technology of the personal computer, and this is a technology that only a small proportion of the world's population enjoys or has any immediate prospect of enjoying. While everything that has been said so far is true of many citizens of North America and Western Europe, it is far from true of all the citizens in these places, still less true of Eastern Europe, and hardly true at all in, say, Africa, the Indian subcontinent or Central Asia. If power to the people depends on the technology of the Internet, then it is a long way off for most of the world's people.

Though it is correct to say that, to date, access to the Internet is available to a relatively privileged few, it would be a mistake in my view to make much turn on this point. We know from other instances that popular technology can spread very quickly and make its appearance in even poor places with surprising rapidity and extent. There was a time, for instance, when expense limited the technology of the transistor radio to small areas of the globe. Now, transistor radios are ubiquitous and in very many places have come to have no greater status than that of a disposable good. It is a marked feature of popular technology that there is a powerful and constant downward pressure on price and hence a constant tendency for the cost of obtaining it to fall. This results in part because its popularity creates a huge demand which manufacturers are ever willing to supply and in part because the innovatory technology which gave rise to it in the first place does not then cease to innovate but sets itself to find ever simpler and more cost-effective ways of doing the same thing or better. This phenomenon is plainly observable in the case of printing, motor transport, refrigeration, television and the telephone. So we should expect the same outcome for computers and the Internet. Indeed the evidence is that this is happening is all about us, and it is surprising in what remote and relatively poor corners of the world it is already to be found. In trying to make some assessment of the implications of the Internet, which this book aims to do, it would be foolish to assume anything other than that its extent will grow in just the way that radio and television have.

If so, and if the philosophical analysis of democracy and the description of the Internet are as I have suggested, we can expect a significant impact on the political processes of democratic states and, in so far as we regard political forms as making up one of the central elements of human life, we may thus conclude that human life is on the edge of a transformation. What we cannot conclude, without further argument, is that this transformation is a transformation to the good, because such a further implication requires that we give unqualified approval to the democratic ideal. Should we do so?

The value of democracy

I remarked at the outset of this chapter that it is difficult to get the question 'Is democracy a good thing?' taken seriously. This is true only of the modern period, however. For most of the time that people have thought about politics, democracy was feared rather than admired because it came close to the appalling state (though wonderful word) of 'ochlocracy' – rule by the mob. From Plato in the fifth century BC to John Stuart Mill in the nineteenth century AD, political theorists have variously denounced or entered serious reservations against democracy as a form of government.

In the modern period, it seems, all such reservations have been set aside. This is not to say that the theory of democracy goes undiscussed. It is often discussed, and in that discussion very many problems and paradoxes have been detected in attempts to formulate and justify the fundamental principles of the democratic ideal. But there is, as it seems to me, an unspoken assumption in almost all modern discussion of these problems that they have and must have a solution, even if satisfactory solutions are not yet forthcoming. It is supposition which I propose to question. Since the topic of democracy and its foundations is a very large one, however, and since I am concerned with it here only in so far as it bears upon the significance of the Internet, I shall limit myself to outlining some of these problems and then focusing upon just two which are specially pertinent to the concerns of this book.

First of the problems facing the theory of democracy is the question of its definition. We owe to Abraham Lincoln the famous formulation 'government of the people, by the people, for the people', but who are 'the people'? One initially plausible suggestion is that 'the people' are all those who are subject to the laws within a given state. Given this conception, the fundamental principle of democracy can be formulated as 'Let those who are subject to the law, make the law'. This certainly captures an influential thought, one which extends the role of law-making far beyond the confines of a traditional, usually hereditary, ruling class. It also subverts a much older idea that there are 'natural' masters and 'natural' servants, and that the latter should be subject to the rule of the former. Instead, it makes the ruling class subject to the will of the ruled, such that governments become the servants and not the masters of the people they govern.

Yet however attractive and admirable these ideas may be, they encounter a difficulty known as 'the problem of inclusion'. To begin with, though the principle 'Let those who are subject to the law, make the law' seems plausible, we need to ask why we should adopt it. One answer might be this: everyone who is affected by laws and public policies has a right to some say in what they should be. Again this seems plausible, but it sustains a rather different principle, namely, 'Let all those who are affected by the law, make the law'. Now since laws and economic policies approved in one country can have an adverse affect upon the citizens of another country, the class of people affected by any sets of laws and policies can be considerably larger than the set of people legally subject to them. Laws relating to political asylum or immigration are cases in point. Who then, does the democratic ideal bid us include among 'the people'?

Even if we found good reason to restrict the application of democracy to the first principle and could ignore the fact that people outside the scope of the law may yet be affected by it, there is a further difficulty. There are classes of people – children, the mentally impaired, resident aliens – who are subject to the law but who cannot, in virtue of their age, ability or origins, be accorded a place in the democratic process. Small children and the mentally impaired (let us leave resident aliens aside) do not have the necessary intellectual equipment to play a proper part in political activity, yet they are subject to the laws that others make and it is difficult to see how it could be otherwise. Their exclusion must be based, therefore, upon another intuitively plausible principle – 'Let those who are sufficiently able to make the law, make the law'. Once we pay serious attention to this restriction, however, it becomes difficult to limit it. We know that adult voters can be ignorant, indifferent or partisan, and that their ignorance and partisanship can tell against their ability to take into account the various, often complex, facts and conditions which good political decision-making requires. How can we consistently exclude children or the mentally impaired on the grounds that they are intellectually ill-equipped to deal with political issues intelligently and responsibly without excluding others who, on other grounds, are no better equipped?

This second problem is connected with the original problem of inclusion, but it has wider ramifications. It raises doubts about another familiar element in the democratic ideal, commonly known as 'one man, one vote'. It was the jurist Jeremy Bentham who (in a different context) coined the slogan 'Each to count for one, and none for more than one'. But why should each count for one? Why should the vote of those who have taken the trouble to inform themselves as best they can about the candidates in an election and the policies for which they stand count for no more than the vote of someone who is ignorantly mistaken about the issues, who whimsically votes according to hair colour or refuses to cast a vote for a candidate from a racial minority regardless of their views? Queen Victoria remarked on one occasion: 'These are trying moments and it seems to me a defect in our much-famed Constitution to have to part with an admirable govt like Lord Salisbury's for no question of any importance, or any particular reason, merely on account of the number of votes'. She had, in my view, a point, and the point is this: there can be rational voting and irrational voting. The exclusion of children and the mentally impaired recognizes this, but the democratic ideal of universal and equal suffrage discounts it. It makes everything turn on numbers.

A third important problem arises with respect to voting as a decision procedure. Who should represent us? What should the law be? In response to both questions the democratic ideal answers: whichever has majority support. Combined with 'government by the people' and 'one man, one vote' this third principle, 'majority rule', may be said to make up the fundamental elements of the democratic ideal. Yet here too there are obvious and important objections to be raised. No less widespread in the modern world than a belief in democracy, is a belief in fundamental human rights, rights which every constitution and legal jurisdiction ought to respect. It does not take much reflection to see, however, that as a result of open, fair and free elections, the majority of an electorate (or the assembly of its representatives) could vote for a law which would violate one of these fundamental rights. Indeed, there are plenty of recorded instances. In such circumstances, what grounds would the believer in rights (or anyone for that matter) have for adhering to the belief in majority rule? To do so would seem once again to be nothing better than the worship of numbers.

Even if we were to find answers to these first three problems, there is a fourth difficulty. This arises from the fact that political life is not static, but part of an historical process. Suppose that there is an election, or a plebiscite, at some point in time which is not subject to the objections we have just been considering. How long does its authority last? The nineteenth-century Chartists, who campaigned for parliamentary reform, included among their demands annual parliaments, that is to say, parliaments which would be elected for one year only. This was widely regarded as impracticable and in Britain, as in all other parts of the world, the time limit (five years) is considerably longer. But, practical considerations aside, is there a 'right' length at all from a democratic point of view? Why should I who, say, was just below the age of voting at the last election, be bound for several years after I reach the approved age by the result of an election or a plebiscite in which I had no part? We can slice electoral periods into whatever lengths we like, there will always be new and competent citizens entering the electorate who will be bound by decisions to which they are subject and by which they are affected and in which they had no part at all. We can certainly fix upon intervals between elections and plebiscites that will be widely accepted as fair and reasonable, but the crucial point is that in-between times *neither* the principle 'Let those who are subject to the law, make the law' *nor* the principle 'Let those who are affected by the law, make the law' can be said to operate. Democracy, it seems, is a form of government that can be realized on occasions, but not over any length of time.

Finally, even supposing this further difficulty could be overcome, wherein lies the justification of either of these two principles? The answer will be found, I think, in another familiar democratic slogan – 'power to the people'. The thought which informs the moral basis of the democracy is that people should have control over their own affairs. This ties in with the Kantian ideal of 'respect for persons'. Since a large part of our lives is determined by law and politics, respect for the autonomy of the individual requires us to accord to individuals some share in shaping the political policies and programmes under which they are required to live. Now thus stated, this thought seems unobjectionable, incontestable perhaps. At any rate I do not propose to contest it. However, there is an important gap between accepting it and inferring from it that democracy has a firm moral foundation. This is because any such inference supposes that democratic foundations do indeed confer a power upon the people who operate them. Is this true?

Power to the people?

In assessing its truth we should bear in mind an important observation. The value of a benefit is not indifferent to the manner of its distribution. Consider this example. We are dividing out emergency supplies of grain and have a fixed amount to distribute. There are many hungry people badly in need of it, let us suppose, and no one has any better claim to a portion than anyone else. It seems to stand to reason that the grain should be divided equally among all those in need. However, the more widely we distribute it, the less each recipient receives. This much is obvious, but what may be less obvious is that, past a certain point, the shares become so small that they are not worth having since they neither assuage hunger nor make any nutritional difference. Distribution past this point is not the sharing of a benefit more widely, but its complete dissipation. In short the value of the quantity of grain with which we began is not indifferent to its distribution.

A similar point, it seems to me, can be made with respect to the distribution of political power. In an autocracy all power is concentrated in a single ruler who can, in theory at any rate, effect whatever result they desire. In an oligarchy, where there is a limited ruling class, though the power is distributed among several, it is still sufficiently concentrated to allow a particular group, or the oligarchy as a whole, to effect its will. As power becomes more widely distributed it runs the risk of dissipation to the point at which no one enjoys any real power at all. This point, arguably, is precisely that at which we have democracy.

By way of demonstration that this is not merely a theoretical possibility, but something actualized in most democracies, consider the following important observation. In an election where the following conditions prevail – every vote counts equally, there are large numbers of voters and the result is decided by majority – it makes no difference which way any given individual votes. If the red candidate wins even by a small majority, then the red candidate would have won whether my vote was cast for red or blue. My vote made no difference to the result. What is true of me, however, is true of every other voter, from which it follows that *no one's* vote made any difference. Even in the very rare case where the outcome was decided by a single vote, this is still true, because there is no reason to identify any actual vote as the crucial one. Only if mine is the last vote and I know that there is a tie does my vote make any difference, and of course a further feature of modern democracies – the secret ballot – rules this out.

It is sometimes hard to accept this as an important problem rather than a paradoxical puzzle. After all, everyone voted knowingly and intentionally, and their votes combined produced a result. How can it be, then, that none of it made any difference? The important distinction to grasp, however, is the difference between a procedure which produces an outcome, and a procedure by which one outcome is chosen in preference to another. There is no doubt that elections based on (near) universal franchise produce outcomes. But so too does tossing a coin. In the case of tossing a coin it is plain that the outcome is not chosen; it is merely decided. This is less plain in the case of an election, but it is in fact the case. A popular election produces an outcome, but it does not enable anyone to choose the result. The power to do so is dissipated by its distribution. What this argument shows is that, whatever other merits democratic voting procedures may have, they do not constitute a transfer of power to the people. But if they do not, where does this leave the underlying thought which was supposed to provide the moral basis for democracy? The answer is: it leaves it at an important remove from the system it was supposed to justify.

The Internet and the deficiencies of democracy

We began the section before last with the question 'Is democracy a good thing?' The difficulties in the theory of democracy that have subsequently been rehearsed suggest, contrary to almost universal belief, that there is nothing much to be said in its favour. It requires the deployment of some arbitrary principle of inclusion; it discounts the rational exercise of political responsibility by putting it on a par with the prejudiced and the irrational; it licenses violations of individual rights in the name of majority will; it is applicable occasion by occasion but unsustainable over even very short periods of time; and its claim to give power to the people is an illusion. I believe all of these to be serious and probably insurmountable problems, but I want to consider two of them more closely and to ask whether the technology of the Internet, which at an earlier stage of the argument was called upon to make up the deficiencies of representative democracy, might make a difference at the more fundamental level of the deficiencies of democracy *per se*.

The two problems to be focused on are those concerning irrationality and powerlessness, and we may most usefully begin with the second. One way of expressing the powerlessness of the ordinary voter is this. It seems reasonable to analyse power as follows. If I have the power to do X, then should I choose to do X, X will result. Now the problem we isolated is this. The theory tells us that in a democracy the people can choose their rulers rather than having them imposed upon them. But for any voter, the choice of X in the polling booth does not imply that X will be elected. What is true of any voter is true of all, from which it follows that no one enjoys the power to choose X as ruler or representative.

It might be replied that no one ever thought it did. The democratic theorist only needs to claim that the choice of rulers is a *collective* power of the people. There are doubts to be raised about the idea of a collective choice because choice implies intention and the suggestion that an electorate, or a part of it, has a collective *intention* is mysterious. But let us leave these doubts aside, because the defender of democracy has another line of argument available. In collective decision-making, such as an elections, it is not just the mechanical business of making the decision that matters, but the formation of opinion about how it should be made. This is what makes sense of election campaigns and all that goes into them. In the course of such campaigns there is scope for both individuals and organized groups to exercise influence by all the familiar methods and media. If, as was agreed at an earlier stage in the argument, the efficacy of these means is a function of the technology that is current, then more powerful communicative technology can be expected to increase the influence of ordinary citizens and thus enhance their place in the democratic process. In other words, just as the Internet was seen to make up the deficiencies of representative democracy, so it can be expected to make up the deficiency of democracy at a more fundamental level.

Given all that has been said, this is a persuasive line of thought, and it is certainly true that influencing political outcomes by means of freedom of expression and assembly has always been held to be an important part of democracy without which the ability merely to cast a vote becomes an empty ritual. But does it really meet the challenge we have been considering? In part 'Yes' and in part 'No', I am inclined to say. This is because equal freedom of expression for all citizens does not imply equal influence. The impact of one form can be very different to that of another and the availability of different forms depends on more than equal freedom. For example, television advertising has a far greater impact on many more people than the door-to-door distribution of poorly produced leaflets. Those who have access to the former will have a much greater degree of influence on the outcome of elections and referenda than the latter, even though both are accorded equal freedom of political expression.

'Precisely', a democrat who was enthusiastic about the Internet might reply. The advantages of the Internet for democracy lie just here. As was observed earlier, both e-mail and web pages place in the hands of relatively ordinary people powers of communication and presentation which have hitherto been the preserve of the relatively wealthy. So we may expect that, along with other related developments such as interactive television, the Internet will increase the political influence of ordinary citizens and thus not only level the political playing field, but close the gap between power and influence which the critic of democracy detects.

Now since I have myself identified some important features of the Internet which support this contention, it would seem perverse to reject this line of response altogether. There are however two important caveats to be entered. The first is that at present there is good evidence to think that relative wealth shows itself on the Internet as much as in any other medium. The quality of the web pages of commercial advertisers is noticeably greater than that of most small groups and individuals. This is likely to remain the case and in so far as difference in quality makes for difference in impact, the inequalities evident in previous forms of political expression – television, billboards, newspaper advertisements and so on – is likely to be replicated on the Internet. This observation does not take account, it is true, of the advantages attributable to e-mail, and for this reason it would be foolish to be overly sceptical and deny that there is the real possibility that the Internet may make an important difference to political participation within a democratic framework.

The second caveat is perhaps more telling. If it is true that the Internet provides unprecedented scope for the expression and presentation of opinion, something of the phenomenon of the dissipation of benefits swings into view. As television channels have multiplied, the amount of public attention that each can hope to command has diminished, with the result that the benefit of being able to broadcast has been reduced just as it has been extended. So too we may reasonably suppose with the Internet. As the quantity of information and material presented on it grows, the amount of attention that any one site can be expected to attract will decrease and hence the value of the medium will fall. This is true of e-mail no less than web pages. Cheapness and convenience may make it easier for ordinary people to express their opinions to newspapers, radio and television stations, or government public-relations desks. But as more messages pour in, in ever larger numbers, the chance of any one of them surfacing significantly falls.

These considerations suggest that the democrat's expectations for the Internet to enhance the democratic process by increasing the influence of ordinary citizens may be over-optimistic. But it is not a point I want to stress unduly. On the best estimate, we may say, the deficiencies of democracy as a way of transferring power to the people may be mitigated to a marked degree by the technology of the Internet, but they will not be eliminated altogether. It remains to ask whether the Internet has any potential solutions to offer with respect to the second problem I proposed to focus on – the indifference of universal suffrage to the rationality of the voter.

The problem here, it will be recalled, is that the ideal of 'one man, one vote' and, for that matter, the ideal of equal freedom of political expression for all citizens, take no account of whether the opinions expressed or the votes cast are grounded in reason or unreason, knowledge or ignorance, prejudice or impartiality. At first sight it might be supposed that the extension of the Internet addresses this problem also. As more information both about facts relevant to political issues and about the opinions of others becomes more easily and more widely available, so we may expect a better informed public and hence higher degree of political deliberation among citizens at large. Whether such a speculation can be anything more than a pious hope is doubtful, in my view. There is, however, more substantial reasoning to be set against it, reasoning based on the nature of the Internet.

Although in superficial respects not unlike television (it uses audiovisual display), the Internet is importantly different. The material on it is not really broadcast; rather it is stored there and, unlike a television programme, remains continuously available until and unless it is removed. In an earlier chapter I compared it to a vast library, picture gallery, shopping arcade and other similar parallels. Such parallels suggest that, rather than tuning in to it, a more adequate image is that of moving round it, and just as in a gallery or a library we stop at and return to those things which most interest us, so too with the Internet. In other words what we give attention to on the Internet is a much more highly selective matter than it is in the case of television. Whereas with television if we do not like or are not interested in what we see on any channel at any given time, our only choice is to turn it off, on the Internet we can go on surfing till we find something that we do like. Now what this means is that there is a built-in tendency for the Internet to favour those whose disposition is not to wander into realms which challenge or conflict with their interests and opinions, but who like their existing interests to be satisfied and their current opinions to be confirmed. Moreover, its interactive character allows for mutual reinforcement in a way that television does not. I do not mean to suggest that there are no genuine inquirers on the Net or that no one ever learns anything new there. This would plainly be absurd. What I do mean to suggest is, first, that information cannot be guaranteed to check or correct the ideas of anyone who comes across it since they may so easily pass on by and, second, that misinformation may be powerfully reinforced as like seeks like. The full implications of this claim will be explored in the next chapter. Here the point is only to observe that there is no reason to expect the Internet, or its further development, to act as a check upon irrational political opinion and behaviour in a democracy. On the contrary, irrationality may be reinforced.

For this same reason, the idea that greater communication across the Internet will lead to the formation of more widespread consensus within the *polis*, one of the ideas with which the last chapter ended, is also something of a pious hope in my view. Just as likely, possibly more likely, is greater fragmentation, a fragmentation that there is reason to call anarchic. This brief remark signals the start of a new topic, one to be explored at length in the next chapter in fact. For the moment, however, it is enough to record that yet again the hopes a democrat might place in the advent of the Internet seem over-optimistic. Widespread consensus is only one possible outcome of political debate; anarchy is another. Before passing on to this new topic, however, it may be useful to summarize the conclusions we have reached about the potential role of the Internet in a democracy.

This chapter has been concerned with some of the problems faced by the democratic ideal, an ideal that has won almost universal and largely unquestioning acceptance. We have seen that despite this acceptance, these problems are both real and deep. There are two which the innovative technology of the Internet might plausibly be thought to address. The first is the gap between the ideal of popular democracy and the representative systems which reality requires us to adopt as, so to speak, a second best. It is reasonable to think that the more effective system of communication and platform for expression which together e-mail and the Internet give us, provide a powerful instrument with which to enter and influence political debates both among the public at large and within political assemblies.

The need to fill this gap and the desirability of being able to do so are matters for the most part taken for granted. Yet, as we have seen, they rest upon an assumption that democracy *per se* is something to be prized and this is an assumption there is good reason to question. In fact, democracy (as its critics in the past have alleged) is a system which prefers equality over rationality in the conduct of political affairs, sanctions an absolute rule of the majority which can be no less tyrannous than that of the greatest autocrat, and disperses power in a way that leaves 'the people' deluded if they think they have become their own political masters.

On this last point democracy can recover some ground by focusing once more on the importance of influence as well as power. In a free society the role of the citizen extends beyond the ballot-box or referendum into the realms where political opinions are formed and particular causes are advanced. Access to this sphere of influence is just as important a part of democracy as the direct exercise of the power to vote, and it is a sphere to which the technology of the Internet gives increased access for ordinary citizens as more immediate and effective means of communication and expression become more widely available. In this way the technology of the Internet may be expected to ameliorate one major deficiency in democracy – its illusion of popular power.

But the same technology does nothing to address the second major problem for democratic theory – its preference for equality over rationality. Democratic theorists tend to assume that the more widely information is disseminated, and the larger the forum for public discussion and debate, the more likely it is that a broad consensus will emerge on major social, moral and political questions. This is an assumption which it is hard to defend. Debate and discussion may as easily uncover differences as commonalities, differences which would have remained dormant had it not been for the process of public debate itself. However this may be, there is reason to ask whether the emergence of consensus in the wider forum to which citizens have increasing access could be the Internet, because by its very nature it has a tendency to promote reinforcement of interest and opinion among the like-minded. In so far as we can speculate about its future, then, there is reason to think that the Internet is more likely to increase social fragmentation than it is likely to promote social consensus. Indeed, there is some reason to take seriously a seemingly more alarming contention – that the Internet will lead to moral anarchy. This is the subject to which we now turn.

5   The Internet as anarchy

It seems that in exploring the implications of the Internet we have been brought from one extreme to another. Having started the last chapter with the optimistic view that it might be the means to a truly democratic society, we are starting this one with the pessimist's contention that the Internet is more likely to produce anarchy. Such an interpretation of the course of our inquiry would be a distortion, however. The argument of the last chapter showed that democracy is not the unqualifiedly admirable ideal it is usually made out to be. If this is correct, then the failure of the Internet to realize democracy in a new and more vibrant form is not failure *per se* and the 'optimism' that it could be expected to do so is misplaced, not because it rests upon futuristic speculation but because of substantial philosophical difficulties surrounding the democratic ideal. In a similar fashion, it is important to see that to predict anarchy as an outcome of the Internet is rightly described as 'pessimism' only if anarchy is a condition to be abhorred. Perhaps the unfavourable view we generally take of anarchy is no better grounded than the unquestioningly favourable view we generally take of democracy.

Positive and negative anarchy

In fact the idea of 'anarchy' can be understood in two ways, one positive and one negative, and both understandings make their appearance in political philosophy. Within the positive conception, the conception of famous anarchists such as Proudhon and

Kropotkin, anarchy means absence of government, and absence of government means freedom from the coercive power of the state. It is for this reason that it is to be welcomed: anarchy is freedom. No less than the positive, the negative (and more commonplace) use of 'anarchy' also denotes the absence of government. But it construes this as a condition of lawlessness, a regime not of liberty but of licence, to use a distinction John Locke (1632–1704) draws in his *Second Treatise of Government*. In short, both the positive and negative conceptions of anarchy have the same descriptive basis – society without the state – but while one regards this as a condition to be welcomed the other regards it as a condition to be feared.

Which view should we take? The arguments in favour of anarchy as a positive ideal have rarely been given serious philosophical exploration, perhaps because as a political ideal it is widely thought to be self-evidently unrealistic. Yet there is at least this to be said in the positive anarchist's favour: the most powerful instrument of human misery, both in times past and in modern times, has been the state. No criminal fraternity or anarchistic conspiracy has ever come close to creating the degree of terror and suffering that was possible through the agency of the state under Stalin, Hitler, Mao or Pol Pot, and these are examples from only one short period of history. Is it really true that societies without states would be worse than societies with states like these?

The opponents of anarchy, those who use the word with negative connotations, might reply that we should not judge the merits of the state by its worst exemplars. They might also concede that the coercive state is indeed undesirable, in theory, but contend that it is a *necessary* evil, in much the same way that radical surgery, for instance, is a necessary evil: no one wants to lose a leg, but better this than the spread of gangrene. This is a familiar line of argument, one to be found, famously, in Thomas Hobbes. The idea is that the state, defined as the monopolist of legitimate coercion, is needed to prevent a constant war of all against all, to establish and prosecute justice, and to protect the innocent and vulnerable.

The positive anarchist might in turn retort that this contention begs the question. It is a solid and sobering fact that the apparatus of the state, whatever its theoretical purpose, can itself be used to perpetrate injustice, to exploit the vulnerable and to injure the innocent. When this happens its effective monopoly on coercion makes matters worse. State terrorism and oppression are far more damaging to the individual and society than anything marauding gangs or even mafias can manage. The anarchist's question then is whether it is wise to call into existence or to maintain an institution whose corruption is so devastating.

The principal purpose of this chapter is not to resolve the argument between anarchists and the defenders of the state. What the preceding paragraphs show is, first, that the prospect of anarchy can be viewed in two different ways and, second, that those who regard it positively are not without some foundation for their view. These observations are merely a preliminary to making some headway with the central question that concerns us here, namely, 'Does the emergence of the Internet constitute a step in the direction of anarchy?' If so, we must ask in which sense of anarchy this is before we know whether to welcome or fear it.

The internationalism and populism of the Internet

In addition to characteristics already discussed, the Internet has two striking features: its internationalism and its populism. The internationalism of the Internet lies not merely in the fact that it connects people across nations, for many human devices and activities do this. The point is rather that the use and exploration of the Internet is wholly *indifferent to* international boundaries. People who are otherwise strangers are linked by common interests which have nothing to do with nationality. In this respect the Internet is to be contrasted sharply with what philosophers call 'civil society', whose characteristic is that it connects strangers by uniting them within one political rule or realm.

For this reason if for no other the Internet has the potential to be politically subversive. The form of this subversion is deep, however. It is not simply that spies and the like now have a near undetectable form of communication with their political masters (which may be true and important) or that terrorists can swap information in relative security (also a real cause for anxiety), but that all the interactions on the Net take place without regard to national boundaries. Since the world of international relations hitherto has largely been a matter of relations between states, what this means is that there is a burgeoning sphere of contact and collaboration over which states, *even in concert*, exercise little or no control. This is true at present. Whether it must remain so is the subject of a later chapter. For the moment, however, we can record that the Internet is largely unregulated and uncontrolled by the state, and since the authority of the state, though not identical with its power, indirectly rests upon that power, the potential for the Internet to diminish the power of the state by creating spheres of activity indifferent to it, is at the same time a potential to diminish the authority of government. It is for this reason that an anarchist (in the positive sense) might welcome it and others fear it.

The second feature of the Internet is its populism. By this I do not mean 'popularity'. The Internet is certainly popular, but its *populism* lies in the fact that access to it is unconstrained except by technical equipment and know-how, equipment the cost of which is falling and know-how that is becoming ever easier to acquire. Again, it is important to see that the populism of the Internet, no less than its internationalism, occurs at a deep rather than a superficial level. As things stand there are no credentials required for exploring it or, more importantly, for contributing to it, and no real system of censorship which would screen contributions in the absence of such credentials. Forms of censorship have been proposed, certainly, though none has yet been effective. Generally, however, these have a specific purpose – the restriction of pornographic materials for example – and are not aimed at a general constraint on or control of access. In fact most government initiatives in information technology are aimed at *increasing* access by making networked computers widely available in schools and colleges. Commercial forces are at work in the same direction. All over the world companies and organizations are encouraging, and paying for, their employees to acquire the requisite skills, and with the institution of the Internet café (an innovation with a limited life in my view: who will bother to go to a café when they can access the Internet from home?) the costs of using and adding to the Internet are so reduced that, far from denting the populism of the system, they intensify it.

It is this populist character that brings cheer to the anarchist, for it seems to present the possibility of a new international order in which the most humble can have unrestricted access to a world of information, communication, interaction, creativity and expression, and by means of which, no less importantly, they can contribute directly to the formation of that world. People on the Internet can say what they like and as they like. They interact and form alliances in accordance with their own individual interests and choices. They exchange information and pursue whatever inquiries and investigations they choose. Their freedom to do all this is unconstrained by national boundaries or the laws of states. The final realization of positive anarchy is complete once we add to this picture the image of frustrated governments looking on, helpless to prevent or regulate, despite all their coercive powers.

To the mind that regards anarchy as a condition to be feared, the very same features of the Internet which the anarchist praises might be thought to be its defects. The Internet is the perfect fomenting ground for criminal conspiracies, for example, and by allowing unrestricted access to every type of interest and activity it calls forth the lowest common denominators of human motivation. The dispute between positive and negative conceptions of anarchy can thus be seen to run very deep. Both acknowledge the ability of the Internet to extend the knowledge and freedom of individuals beyond social and political control, but while the first regards such knowledge and freedom as a source of good, the second regards them as a source of harm and possibly evil.

Both the scenarios envisaged here, though certainly not fanciful, make two assumptions which there is good reason to examine. The first is that the Internet is marked by unrestricted flow of information, and allied to this is the unspoken supposition that knowledge is power, a topic touched upon earlier. The second assumption is that freedom consists in the untrammelled pursuit of personal interest and preference. Only if this is so can we regard the ability to surf the Net with regard to nothing but one's own desires as either a sphere of liberty or licence.

Knowledge and 'information'

The first of these assumptions is connected with at least one of the issues discussed in previous chapters, namely, the role of information (and hence influence) in the political process. But there are other aspects of it which will bear further examination. There is a naivety sometimes evident in enthusiasts for the Internet, especially educationalists and others those who may know relatively little about it. This lies in their easy assumption that in the Internet we have a vast storehouse of information. The assumption is misleadingly sustained by the technical use of the term 'information'. In the expression 'digital information' the word 'information' is used in its barest sense and means no more than a set of electronic impulses which can be made to produce text and images on a screen. Information in this technical sense has no epistemological implications: it does not imply that such information conveys any genuine knowledge. This is what makes it misleading, because in normal speech 'information' *is* an epistemologically normative term: to be newly possessed of information implies that we now know something we did not know before. But 'digital information' can store *misinformation* in the ordinary sense as much as it can store the truth, so that the text or image it generates may be wholly misleading and produce erroneous belief rather than knowledge.

The confusion of digital information with information properly so-called leads to another naivety: that the Internet is authoritative in the way that libraries and information services normally are. This is a mistake that schoolchildren and students are led to make when they are taught to regard the Internet as a 'resource' which may be of use to them in their studies. To 'find' something on the Internet is not like finding something in the *Encyclopaedia Britannica*. Wherein lies the difference? It lies in the fact that the *Encyclopaedia Britannica* has been constructed for a certain purpose, comes from an identifiable source and has a long history by which it has been accredited. None of this is true of the Internet as such, which contains what it contains for every and any purpose and comes from any and every source, identifiable and unidentifiable. Of course, there are things like the *Encyclopaedia Britannica* to be found there, but it is plainly illicit to infer from the fact that some sites on the Internet are authoritative to the conclusion that the Internet as such carries epistemological authority. It does not.

What this shows is that we must be careful not to confuse the power of the Internet as a form of communication with its value as a conveyer of (epistemologically significant) information. It would amount to wild disregard for what we know about human beings to ignore this distinction. All the undeniable advantages of the Internet make it as powerful an instrument for deception and misinformation as for knowledge and learning.

How are we to secure the latter while avoiding the former? The most obvious answer is that we should treat the Internet in precisely the same way that we treat every other medium. We regard some newspapers and broadcasting stations as more reliable than others, the statistics produced by some governments as more trustworthy than others, the research and reports of some agencies as better based than others. Almost all such judgements are made on the strength of previous knowledge and acquired reputation. If I read in a newspaper known for its sensationalism that 'scientists' in Tashkent (say) have discovered the site of a Martian landing, I will treat the claim with scepticism. If I read in the *Washington Post*, or *The Times* in London, that physicists at MIT believe an important step has been taken in the direction of cold fusion, I will treat the report with respect, however surprising I may think the suggestion to be. The difference is not, as some 'postmodernists' would have us believe, a matter of prejudice or convention which arbitrarily favours some sources over others. Although I cannot myself go to Tashkent and inspect the evidence, and would have little understanding of the basis upon which the claim about cold fusion is made even if presented with it first hand, previous knowledge tells me that some newspapers are indifferent to accuracy provided only that they can run an eye-catching headline and reputation tells me that MIT is a serious scientific establishment. All this amounts to good reason to discount the former report and give a measure of credence to the latter.

Such considerations do not settle the matter. It could be that there really is evidence of a Martian landing in Tashkent, and even sober scientists at MIT can get carried away; cold fusion has proved a beguiling prospect in the past. But in these examples, as in almost every other, the only guide we have to reasonable belief is probability; proof is a very rare commodity. The important point to be emphasized here, though, is that such probability judgements cannot be read off from the newspaper reports; they must be made in the light of what we already know in a wider context.

So too with the Internet. What we find there is of value from the point of view of knowledge and reliable information only in so far as we are able to check it against things that we know from elsewhere. If I call up on the Internet the official timetable of SNCF, the French railway company, I have every reason to think that the train times I find there can be relied upon. I know this, not because of anything about the Internet itself, but because of my prior knowledge of the status and established purpose of SNCF, which, to repeat, is not to say that there is no possibility of being misinformed by what I find there. Official timetables published in good faith can contain errors.

The somewhat extravagant picture of the Internet as both a storehouse and exchange of valuable information untrammelled by the intrusions of governments obsessed with secrecy and preserving a monopoly on the power that knowledge brings, is a not unpleasing version of the anarchist's dream. But it is nonetheless a serious misrepresentation. The Internet is a valuable source of knowledge and information only in so far as we are able to subject what we find on it to all the normal checks we customarily use in the case of other sources, and neither its size, nor the freedom of the individual to access it, alters this. In short, material on the Internet is as reliable and as unreliable as the sources from which it comes.

The Internet, then, is not, properly speaking, a source of information at all, but only a medium. Interestingly, though, the nature of the medium may itself undermine its value as a source of information. Indeed, it can be argued that the feature which makes the Internet remarkable – total freedom of access – is the very feature that does this. In the examples we have been exploring, an important part of sifting the probable from the improbable was seen to lie in assessing the trustworthiness of the source. In turn this requires that such a source be identifiable and this means identifiable in contexts other than its appearance on the Internet. This is not always possible, and is markedly not possible in the case of single individuals. It can be done and has been known for individuals to create a wholly false or imaginary persona on the Internet, and to fool other users into thinking that what they are encountering and engaging with is a real person with a distinctive set of beliefs and interests.

The full significance of this possibility is a topic for a later stage in the argument, but there is a point of some consequence to be made here. Imagine that I come across a site on the Internet that purports to be that of a doctor living and practising in California. I engage in 'conversation' and we exchange personal information and opinions. A 'friendship' develops and I regularly call up the site to find out what's new in California and the world of American medicine. Provided only that the exchange is regular and coherent enough, I could easily come to believe that I had a valuable source of information, and might relate to other friends 'facts' about the weather there or about a strange and hitherto unknown disease which has recently been detected. Yet there is nothing in this scenario so-described that is inconsistent with my 'Californian doctor friend' being the invention of a former radio ham only three streets away.

It is not difficult to imagine this example multiplied and all the imaginary personae interlinked such that a wholly imaginary set of people comes into existence. At this point, the one genuine user is caught up in a world of unreality, and its unreality lies in the fact that it is unconstrained by any external check against some other knowledge of the identity of its source. Whether what we have here is the beginning of 'virtual' reality is a topic for a later chapter. For the present, it is enough to observe that this evident possibility throws a different light on the conception of the Internet as a medium of communication and exchange which, by permitting a flow of information unrestricted by governments, can be expected to provide the knowledge which will empower ordinary citizens. For in their engagements with other 'citizens', individual surfers are also at risk of being swept into a world of fantasy and delusion.

It would be wrong to say that the one is *just as* likely as the other. What the chances are is impossible to estimate. Probably the vast majority of sites on the Internet which are not independently identifiable are nonetheless genuine and will remain so. But the point is that exchanges freely entered into on the Internet and without state interference cannot be *assumed* to be real exchanges which increase the knowledge and hence the power of the individual citizen.

Knowledge as power

' ... and *hence* the power ... ' – is this a legitimate inference anyway? The familiar slogan 'knowledge is itself power' comes from Francis Bacon (1561–1626), one of the most influential figures in the development of empirical science, whose thoughts on technology we have already encountered briefly. But is it true and, if so, in what spheres is it true? It is not difficult to imagine circumstances in which knowing something can make an important difference to our ability to act, and being kept in ignorance can render us relatively powerless. But we cannot generalize from the existence of such circumstances to the universal doctrine that knowledge is power. Sometimes it is and sometimes it isn't. Although 'knowledge' is an honorific term, the fact is that we can have genuine knowledge of things that are trivial and worthless, not *worth* knowing. Conversely, as I observed in an earlier chapter, it is also the case that coming to know about matters of great moment may leave us frustrated precisely because we there is nothing we can do about them. At the height of the conflict in Bosnia, steps were taken to prevent the Muslim minority in Serbia from broadcasting details of their plight. The Internet came to the rescue and, despite the best efforts of the Serbian authorities, important information about what was happening reached the West. This was heralded in some quarters as evidence of the power of the Internet to act as a voice of the oppressed which no amount of armed might could silence. Yet, for all that, those who received the information were able to do little to assist. They learnt of real horrors, but their knowledge brought no relevant power. Something of the same might be said about television and the famous pictures of

Tiananmen Square which appeared around the world so rapidly at the time of the student revolt. We *knew* about it, but could *do* nothing.

It is important not to overstate either side of the case here. It may be that in very many cases the freedom of the Internet increases the knowledge and understanding of ordinary people in ways that would not have happened hitherto, and that this makes a considerable difference to the degree of control they exercise over their own affairs, including the political and social affairs by which they are affected. Such has certainly been true of the printing press. Nevertheless, as the example of the printing press amply demonstrates, there are limits to the degree to which this is likely to happen. The difference with the Internet is supposed to lie in its ability to escape political control, which printing cannot do or cannot do to the same extent. But, as we have seen, the Internet can aid deception as well as the communication of (real) information, so that it is as useful for publicizing the trivial and the false as it is for disclosing the important and the true. These internal features are sufficient to place limits on its value, irrespective of the degree to which it is subject to state control.

There are, then, important reservations to be made about the anarchist's hopes regarding the Internet's advantages for the spread of information, the propagation of knowledge and the power which this puts in the hands of ordinary people. However, these reservations are logically consistent with the claim that the limits which the Internet generates internally are far less restricting than those which state control has placed on all previous forms of communication, and with the further claim that they are of no real practical consequence. The freedom of the Internet is not unlimited, that is to say, but in practice the limits may be unlikely to confine the intelligent user to any significant degree. This, it should be noted, is an empirical claim about how the Internet works in fact and a speculation about how it will work out in the future. Such a claim about the present state of play is hard to assess and such speculation about the future is imponderable. It is true, however, that one possible outcome as the Internet develops is that its character as a medium of exchange in knowledge and information free from state intervention and regulation greatly outweighs its internal capacity for propagating misinformation and delusion. Suppose that this *possible* outcome is the *actual* outcome. Would we then have reason to think that the positive vision of anarchy was at last being realized or would we have reason to be alarmed at the approach of anarchy in the negative sense? This brings us to the second assumption outlined at the start – that freedom consists in the untrammelled pursuit of personal interest and preference.

Freedom and reason

Philosophers have written at very great length on the concept of freedom. The simplest conception of freedom is the uninhibited pursuit of desire. I am free, that is to say, if I can get what I want without external hindrance. This is the conception of freedom we find in Thomas Hobbes (1588–1679). Set against it is the contention of Immanuel Kant (1724–1804) that action which is merely driven by felt desire is not free, that people can be enslaved to internally generated desire no less than to external forces. On this second conception, freedom of action properly so-called must have its origins in reason: only rational action is properly called free.

Behind this disagreement lie very large issues in moral psychology and the philosophy of mind which cannot be settled or even addressed in a short compass, and which would in any case take us very far from the main issue in hand. It is inevitable, therefore, that what can usefully be said here must fall short of an adequate treatment of the question. Still, *something* can be said which will advance our discussion of the implications of the Internet. The first step is to rehearse a few familiar facts of human experience.

The attractiveness of the simple conception of freedom derives in part from the fact that unfreedom can take the form of external restrictions on doing what we want. Imprisonment is an obvious example: I want to leave and I can't. This seems a paradigmatic case of not being free. At the same time, to use this as the basis for a general claim that freedom simply consists in being able to get what we desire seems to conflict with other cases. I might not feel free to say what I think because I do not want to look foolish. If only I cared less about the reactions of other people I would be more free. In this case it seems that the obstacle to my freedom is internal, not external, my desire to avoid embarrassment. Or take this case: I think it would be better for me not to smoke, but on every occasion I try to give up, I give in to the desire for a cigarette. Once again it seems that the obstacle is internal rather than external.

This last example is the sort of case of which the Kantian conception of freedom makes much. The desire to smoke is a felt desire, but it stops me from doing what I think I ought. It seems that an equally paradigmatic case of freedom is being able to do what is in accordance with my considered estimates of what is good and bad, right and wrong. I judge it bad to smoke and if I were truly free I could act on this judgement. But brute desire gets in the way. In this instance, getting what I want – that is, a cigarette – is not an example of freedom but of enslavement, enslavement to my desires. The case, however, is somewhat underdescribed. What we have here is not a straightforward clash between reason and desire because another way of describing the example is to say that while I want a cigarette, I also want to give up smoking. Consequently, on the 'reason' side of the conflict, a desire figures also.

It would be wrong, however, to suppose that this returns us to the simple Hobbesian conception of freedom of action as the untrammelled pursuit of desire. The conflict I have just described may be a conflict between desires, but it is a conflict between what we may call a 'tutored' and an 'untutored' desire. The desire for a cigarette is untutored: I simply experience it as felt. The desire to give up smoking is tutored: it is a result of my having thought about risks and consequences and weighed up the pleasure of smoking against the costs to my health. It seems then that the opposition between reason and desire is too simple. Some of the desires we have, we have precisely because we have engaged in thinking.

Another way of expressing this more sophisticated account is to say that while I *want* to smoke, I would *prefer* to give up. I shall use the word 'preferences' as a generic term for human motivations which have some sort of reflective evaluative component – interest, curiosity, benevolence and so on – as opposed to those that are more brute – hunger, fear, anger and so on. Preferences in this sense, though informed by knowledge and understanding, are not merely deliverances of 'pure' reason. They are rooted in untutored impulses and desires which it is natural for human beings to feel. I shall say, then, that freedom consists in being able to choose according to our preferences. This does not relegate or discount entirely the important element of desire, but it places its motivating force within the larger context of reasoned reflection and deliberation, both of which, after all, are elements in our moral psychology also.

How are desires tutored into preferences? The short answer is 'education', and most education comes about as a result of socialization. Clearly, before socialization has taken much hold, even before it has begun perhaps, there are desires present in human beings and they help to explain their behaviour. New-born babies *want* food and warmth instinctively. The process of socializing may be construed as the refinement of such desires into preferences and, in part at least, this is by means of a process in which basic desires undergo submission to external influences.

Thus, for instance, the desire for vocal utterance is in this sense natural or basic: without it human beings would not acquire language. But the desire to utter sounds is in itself, literally, incoherent: it is only with the acquisition of an inherited and uninvented language that it can become a form of expression. We might say that (almost) everyone has a natural desire to speak, but they must learn how to talk, and learning this means submitting the natural impulse for self-expression to the tutoring discipline of the community of language speakers.

Learning in this sense is socialization, and socialization is sometimes referred to as social conditioning. The two terms are not interchangeable, however. Social conditioning summons up the model of Pavlov's famous dogs – a training of natural impulses by a causal process. Socialization, by contrast, is a process not of conditioning but of *formation*, a process by which natural impulses are shaped, refined and guided. Of course, the fact that this involves a sort of submission can make it seem that 'free' impulses are being confined or tamed. 'Man is born free', the famous opening sentence of *The Social Contract* by Jean-Jacques Rousseau

(1712–78) runs, 'and everywhere he is in chains'. Rousseau's subject is not quite that with which we are concerned here, but the sentence captures a familiar thought – that socialization means confinement and restriction. The thought, however familiar, is nonetheless mistaken. As Kant remarks in a different context, 'The light dove, cleaving the air in her free flight, and feeling its resistance, might imagine that its flight would be still easier in empty space' (Kant, *Critique of Pure Reason*, p. 47). The point is that the pressures which may feel like constraints and restrictions are what make it possible to fly at all. So too with the social forms within which individual action must take place. They do not confine or restrict that which might otherwise be free; they make choice and action possible.

Licence, to return to Locke's distinction, is not liberty unconfined, but the end of liberty. Linguistic forms do not force our natural utterances into the conventionally acceptable. They make it possible for us to converse. Something of the same sort, it seems to me, should be said about morality. Whatever the natural impulses that lie at its heart and, as it were, constitute the active basis of moral consciousness, they gain definition as they are submitted to the refining process of an inherited and uninvented set of values and practices. As I argued earlier, it is a mistake to think that things are valued because they are desired; rather, our desires are fashioned as we tailor them to what we learn, through inherited collective experience, about what is worth desiring, and thus come to have preferences for those things that are valuable. Thus, for example, a taste for music may be a natural desire, but it is a taste which achieves maturity through being fashioned by learning about the musical forms and compositions which collective experience shows to be adequate objects for its realization.

Conceived in this way, moral education is most obvious in the early years of a life, but it continues indefinitely and at every stage its form is the same – the submission and tempering of natural impulses to socializing influences. This is what makes individual freedom possible, but it also has the happy outcome of coordinating the preferences of otherwise disparate human beings, and hence making civilized society possible. In short, the process of socialization is both liberating and integrating, and it is no accident in my view that serious social deviants (notably serial killers) have usually been radically alienated in some respect by their psychological histories.

Moral anarchy and the Internet

One thing that is striking about the Internet is that it allows, even encourages, the formation of what I shall call pure confluences of interest. That is to say, the ability simply to surf a vast unstructured web of material which both expresses and provokes an enormous variety of tastes and interests gives scope to mere congruence rather than coordination. Surfers have the opportunity to seek out kindred spirits and to pass over the sort of reforming and refining influences that operate in normal processes of learning. This is evidenced most strikingly perhaps in such things as child pornography networks where, I shall assert, evil desires are unchecked because those things which would normally check them can be ignored by the surfer and are then strengthened by meeting with reinforcing responses. A taste for such material cannot easily be given public expression in the world at large, and this normally means that it cannot enter into social intercourse. But in the world of the Internet, 'the public' can be disregarded.

Child pornography is an extreme case, but the same point can be made about relatively innocuous examples – the trivial, the bizarre and the ludicrous. These too will find the Internet a medium in which everything that would challenge, check and correct can be side-stepped and everything that would reinforce can be sought and returned to again and again. So, for example, the believer in fairies and poltergeists who turns to the Internet is sure to find psychological confirmation and need pay no attention to scientific criticism, and the self-made philosopher with a grand but completely vacuous 'theory of everything' will sooner or later find a coterie of people whose knowledge and critical acumen is even less, but who are willing to be impressed. This explains why it is possible to find on the Internet large quantities not only of filth but of rubbish.

The logical terminus of such a form of interaction is moral fragmentation rather than moral community, and though the practical upshot is certain to fall short of this logical extremity, the fact that this *is* the logical extension demonstrates the existence of an important and destructive tendency. The 'liberty' of the Internet is tailor-made to encourage a descent into 'licence'. Such fragmentation is anarchic in the bad sense, since it is a means for the release and confluence of untutored desires of any and every kind.

There is good reason to think, of course, that it can never be complete, because a basic level communication is always required – communication requires a language of some sort and in turn this necessitates the submission of untutored impulses to socializing influences in the way previously described. Even those who use the Internet to seek out kindred spirits interested in revelling in the most elemental impulses have to find some way of talking to one another. Moreover, if the conjunction of untutored interests and desires is to result in combined activity (the formation of Internet groups, for example) this itself requires a measure of social order and discipline. In fact, the Net has spontaneously generated its own (limited) code of conduct, a code that has since the mid-1980s been known as 'Netiquette', and of which there seems to be a measure of enforcement.

> Clumsy attempts at Internet advertising [are] referred to as 'spamming' for some inexplicable reason ... Posting advertising messages to all news groups; slogans and messages attached to an otherwise innocuous or even irrelevant posting; all of these have collected their critics, even resulting in a 'blacklist' of advertisers from whom Internet users are encouraged not to buy. The authors of the blacklist even go so far as to give suggestions for a number of mechanisms within the Internet that can be used against such advertisers. The most famous – or infamous – example of spamming is that of the American lawyers Canter & Siegel whose deliberate and celebrated stratagem resulted in a stream of abusive messages and the withdrawal of their Internet access by their then service provider when their computer became overloaded.
>
> (Barrett, *The State of the Cybernation*, p. 81)

But at most 'Netiquette' lays down minimal rules against system abuse. It does nothing to counter the nature of the Internet as a form of communication and exchange which makes possible and encourages a far more widespread release of 'free' spirits, without the civilizing influences which normally harness, refine and constrain them.

In the end, then, it seems that the pessimists are more in the right than the optimists: the Internet has the makings of an anarchic society, but it is anarchy of the bad, not the good, kind. Still, even if the argument and analysis that has led us to this point is sound, such a conclusion may yet seem unduly alarmist. This is for two reasons. First, it is assumed by both the positive and negative views of anarchy that the Internet is not only largely unregulated by the state, but that it is unregulatable. Such an assumption must turn in part on factual questions – questions about what is and what is not technically possible. These are not questions that can be answered once and for all, however. We know that what is technically impossible, even inconceivable, at one time, can become utterly commonplace at another. It would be foolish therefore to let anything important turn on a question of technical possibility. This is especially true of the Internet which, as we have noted many times, is only at the start of its development. Who knows what means may develop by which states, alone or in concert, or society more generally perhaps, are enabled to control and regulate the activities of the individual on the Internet? A priori it is not plausible to think that such means are beyond the reach of technical invention, yet this is just what the claim about the anarchic nature of the Internet does.

Second, even if we set the question of possible technologies aside for the moment (the next chapter will return to it), there is a further assumption at work which ought to be examined. To move from the claim that the Internet is a medium of human interaction with the potential for moral fragmentation to the further claim that there is an actual risk of such fragmentation is to suppose that the Internet is not merely a law but a *world* unto itself, that is a self-contained sphere the character of which is wholly determined by its own nature. But this is false. Internet users are also denizens of the world of houses, shops and hospitals. Suppose it is true that the Internet has an in-built tendency to anarchy in the sense of moral fragmentation. There is no reason to think that this will come to predominate over the forces of social cohesion. So long as the Internet remains only one aspect of modern life, integrated into commerce, education and leisure, there is every reason to suppose that the interactions of those who use it will continue to be tutored and constrained by the normal processes of socialization.

Both these are points well taken, and they give pause to any excessively Neo-Luddite predictions of doom and disaster following in the wake of new technology. On the other hand, they cannot be assumed to be true. Both are claims which warrant further investigation and in fact their investigation provides the subject matter for most of the rest of this book. Is there something essentially unpoliceable about the Internet? And could the Internet become to a large extent a world of its own? The second of these questions admits of a less and a more ambitious answer. One line of inquiry turns on whether the advent of the Internet introduces the possibility of a new social order – a world in which relationships are of a different kind. Another suggestion is that there are deeper, metaphysical possibilities in view. It is to these issues that we now turn.

6   Policing the Internet

Is there something essentially unpoliceable about the Internet? This question is important (and troubling) only if we have reason to believe that the Internet *needs* policing. To show that it does, it is not enough merely to establish that the Internet gives scope to right and wrong, good and bad, which undoubtedly it does. A natural language can be used well or badly and grammatical structures can be right or wrong; these facts alone do not support the contention that the use of natural languages needs to be policed or (*pace* the Académie Française) that there is any point in trying to do so. So why is it that someone might think this about the Internet? The usual answer is that the Internet is a medium for two sorts of material about which society has reason to be especially concerned – the harmful and the pornographic. To what, exactly, do these terms refer?

It is often supposed that we can only answer this question if we *define* 'pornography' and 'harm'. In moral philosophy, however, and philosophy more generally, definitions rarely accomplish much. Their purpose is to capture some phenomenon or other with precision, but most concepts are what has been called 'open-textured' and do not admit of this sort of precision. The result is that almost all such definitions leave out some instances that common usage would include, and not infrequently, if consistently applied, include instances which are contentious. Holding firmly to the definition in the face of these conflicts with ordinary language makes it stipulative and by and large one person's stipulation is as good as another's. As Stephen Toulmin has said in a different context:

Definitions are like belts. The shorter they are, the more elastic they need to be. A short belt reveals nothing about its wearer: by stretching it can be made to fit almost anybody. And a short definition, applied to a heterogeneous set of examples, has to be expanded and contracted, qualified and reinterpreted, before it will fit every case. Yet the hope of hitting on some definition which is at one and the same time satisfactory and brief dies hard.

(Toulmin, *Foresight and Understanding*, p. 18)

However, if the attempt to define a term is of little use in philosophy, the failure to do so is not of any great consequence either. Even in the absence of a precise definition, for the most part we can make clear what it is we are talking about and go on to say something of interest and significance, as the ensuing discussion will show. There is nonetheless an important point to be made about definition in the present context. Policing the Internet (or anything else) usually implies at some point or other the invocation and application of law. Here, by contrast with philosophy, definition – that is, legal definition – can often be crucial. If an offence cannot be specified and defined precisely, the law regulating it is difficult (sometimes impossible) to apply and by the same token relatively easy to evade. We can see this with respect to pornography in Britain. The laws relating to it are framed in terms of the obscene, but the inability to define 'obscenity' with sufficient clarity has made the law relating to pornography so difficult to apply that very few cases now come to court.

Pornography is a topic to be dealt more fully later on. For the moment it is sufficient to note that the possibility (or impossibility) of definition is a matter of much greater moment in law than in morality or philosophy. The law is another topic to be discussed in this chapter, but since it is the moral and philosophical foundations of legal regulation that concern us first, we can defer the issue of definition to a later stage.

Pornography and harm

The Internet contains harmful and pornographic material. At one level this claim is incontestable, but in order to assess whether it amounts to a problem of any great consequence and, if so, what sort of problem it is, some initial clarification is needed. First of all, pornographic and harmful materials are not the same. Objections can be made to pornography *whether or not* it is harmful. Indeed, the claim that it is harmful is usually a refuge for those who, really, think that it is objectionable in itself, but believe that couching their objections in terms of harm is more likely to command agreement. This contention – that pornography is harmful – is familiar, but in reality hard to establish. What is worth noting here is that the fact that there can be disagreement about whether it is or not shows that the pornographic and the harmful are not the same. We have to be able to identify the pornographic independently of its effects (good or bad) before we can isolate those effects. What this shows is that there *could* be objections to pornography that do not rest on claims about the harm it causes. Whether there are, and whether they are the sorts of objection that could justify legal regulation, are important matters to be dealt with at greater length in a subsequent section. For the present, we will stick to the claim about harm.

Pornography tends to dominate discussions about policing the Internet, but there is plenty of material that can be thought of as more immediately harmful – material that might assist terrorists, criminals and social subversives, for example. However, only *some* of this material is harmful properly speaking – software which can damage, destroy, illicitly alter or deploy other people's web pages. Computer viruses are of this nature. But most of the material people worry about is not directly but *potentially* harmful. For example, it is relatively easy to find web sites that provide information on how to make simple explosives, construct timing devices or even obtain nuclear weapons. Such information is in fact harmless, of course, unless it is actually used to make bombs or secure supplies of arms. In advance of these actions, it constitutes a source of potential, not actual, harm. This does not mean that there is no cause to worry about it, but it does raise a further complication.

The chances that *potentially* harmful material becomes *actually* harmful are not uniform; they vary from case to case and this can make a difference to the case for regulation. Material which has a very small chance of generating actual harm is not as convincing a subject for proscription as that for which the chances are high, especially if there is a trade-off between benefits and harms to be considered. To take a different example: the benefits of making a drug available to the public can be outweighed by a serious chance of harmful side-effects, whereas if the chances of the same side effects are very low, the case against allowing it on the market is considerably weaker. The general point is that any social interaction may have a potential for harm, but, precisely because this is so, we cannot eliminate the potentially harmful; we have to engage in risk assessment and management.

These remarks are not much more than preliminaries to the main argument. Still, they do show that the mere fact that pornographic and potentially harmful materials can be found on the Internet is not of itself sufficient to sustain calls for its regulation. Before there is even a case to answer, it must be shown *both* that pornography is intrinsically objectionable *and* that the chances of potential harm becoming actual are reasonably high.

Let us suppose, if only at this point in the argument, that these two important claims can be convincingly substantiated. The question then arises as to how and whether anything is to be done about this. In the last chapter we explored the suggestion that there is something about the Internet which makes it specially suited to a kind of moral anarchy. That is to say it is a medium where the normal social pressures operating to check individual impulses and create a measure of conformity and community are absent or at least seriously diminished. If this is granted, it might be supposed that the principal task is to devise ways in which the operation of the Internet can be controlled and in turn this may be taken to imply, as it usually is, that the main question is a technological one: can the individual's use of the Internet be suitably constrained by (usually) governmental or intergovernmental regulators?

It should be observed at the outset, however, that the question of policing the Internet should not be thought of solely or even primarily as a technical matter. There are technical aspects to it certainly. Is it possible, and if so how, to scrutinize the material that individuals sitting at PCs in the privacy of their own homes choose to put on the Internet and to block it when it transgresses some socially accepted norm? Even if this technical question were answered in the positive, and effective means had been devised (both of which are matters to be considered in the next section) there would remain this question: *which* material should be blocked in this way? This further question calls not for yet more technology but for *judgement* and it is a deep mistake to think that technological devices could take the place of human judgement in this or any other context. This is illustrated by the fact that in several celebrated pornography prosecutions (the trial relating to the publication of D.H. Lawrence's novel *Lady Chatterley's Lover* is one of the most famous) the material in question has been defended on aesthetic grounds – 'It is not pornography but art'. If such a claim constitutes even an a priori defence, we need to be able to discriminate between art and pornography. This is not a discrimination we could ever reasonably expect a technical device to make for us. If we were possessed of such a device (for the Internet) we would have the means to block or eliminate material to which there is objection. But we would still have to decide whether or not to *use* the device and on which items. Neither is a decision that the device itself will take for us.

So much, it seems to me, is acknowledged in such government and intergovernment reports about regulating the Internet as I have been able to read. What this means is that any attempt to police the Internet must address two questions: the question of technical possibility and the question of principles of judgement. There is then the further question of translating these principles of judgement into applicable law. It is these three questions that will provide us with the topics of the next three sections.

Licensing and labelling

Is it technically possible to control what is and is not put on the Internet? This question should not be confused with another closely related one: is it practically possible to do this? What is *technically* possible may make no *practical* difference because it is not, or will not be, deployed. The reasons for this can vary. The technology required might be too expensive, for example; or it is so widely resisted that it does not meet with the general cooperation its successful operation requires; or it proves politically impossible to pass the laws which would license its employment; and so on. All these are obstacles to making the technically possible practicable. In inquiring about the possibilities of policing the Internet we need to be alive to this difference and to address the two issues together. But let us begin with what appears to be the purely technical.

How might we regulate what appears on the Internet? There are a number of suggestions but they break down into two basic strategies. The first seeks to limit or control access to the Internet, the second aims at direct restrictions on content. The most obvious way to tackle the first would be through a system of licensing. To gain access to the Internet from a desktop computer, a user must employ a server – usually an independent Internet Service Provider (ISP). That is to say, individual PCs tap into a system which both connects with the World Wide Web and provides the capacity for storing and processing digital information. Although there is no reason in principle why individuals should not operate from their own servers, the cost and the need for expert maintenance means that almost all servers belong to public institutions, commercial organizations or companies who make their money from the provision of servers to users. Perhaps as the technology develops, personal servers will become more common. Such an eventuality would complicate any system of licensing, but would not in principle make it impossible, any more than it is impossible to require licenses for cars or televisions owned by individuals.

The system would work like any other licensing system. The owner of a server – whether an individual or an organization – would require a licence, and the continued award of such a licence would depend upon certain conditions being satisfied. These conditions could include requirements relating to the material that can and cannot be put on the Web – what is known as 'content management'. If an ISP were found to have permitted harmful or pornographic material to appear, the licence would be revoked in just the way that the driving licence of someone found guilty of careless or dangerous driving can be revoked. Applied to the Internet, the system of licensing could be made stronger if it became technically possible to jam or otherwise disable servers whose owners were known not to have licences. It would be like putting wheel clamps on the cars of those whose driving licences have been revoked. The question arises, of course, about what is to count as illegitimate content, but this raises issues of judgement which are to be addressed in the next section of this chapter.

Would such a system be effective, even assuming some sort of jamming or disabling? The first point to be made in reply is that it is certain to be imperfect. We know this because we know that all existing systems of licensing are imperfect. It is practically impossible to ensure that all and only those entitled to licences have them, and impossible to ensure that only those with licences engage in the activity for which a licence is required. People drive illegally and get away with it, and this would be true even if the wheels on their own cars had been clamped. The proportion of drivers in this category will vary from place to place and time to time depending on a number of factors, including the efficiency of the authorities and the law-abidingness of citizens, but even in the most law-abiding countries with the most efficient authorities there will be illegal activity. So too with the Internet, were the licensing of ISPs to be introduced.

A measure of illegality is unavoidable, therefore, but there are reasons to think that in the case of the Internet it is likely to be considerable. First, the system of licensing ISPs requires two distinct levels of control: the regulation of ISPs by the authorities and the management of content by the ISPs themselves. If a measure of slack is inevitable at the first level, so it is as well at the second, and a reasonable guess would be that it is likely to be greater. This is because at both levels there has to be a system of inspection. Since the number of users will be vastly greater than the number of ISPs, the inspection of users is accordingly more difficult and neither institutions nor commercial companies are likely to have the resources to conduct more than occasional random checks. The degree of slack would be even greater if, as we can suppose, regulation at neither level was wholly draconian.

That is to say, while the rule *could* be that a single instance of for-
bidden material was sufficient to revoke the licence of an ISP or to
exclude a user from the provider's list of customers, it is more
likely that there would be a scale of offence – a 'three strikes and
you're out' policy, say – thereby permitting quite a large number of
occasional improper uses.

We have some experience to use as evidence here. At present
there are copyright and licensing laws which apply to the Internet
as much as to anything else. These relate to software as well as to
text, pictures and so on. Both legal systems and commercial sup-
pliers take steps to enforce such laws, and do so to some effect.
Nevertheless, there is a very considerable amount of unlicensed
software in use and probably even more unlawful use and exchange of copyright material. We have no reason to suppose that
laws relating to the licensing of ISPs or the supply of servers to
users would be any more effective. It is a parallel and a precedent
which, as we will see, illuminates the topic of this chapter in other
respects as well.

There is one further important objection to requiring ISPs to
have licences that they may forfeit, and this is that it punishes
those who have done no wrong. It is an objection that has been
raised against at least one noted prosecution under existing law.
This was the trial and conviction of Felix Somm, former head of
the German subsidiary of CompuServe, one of the world's largest
ISPs. In 1998 Somm was a given a two-year suspended sentence
for spreading violent, animal and child pornography on the
Internet, and ordered to pay £35,000 to charity. He himself had
not actually disseminated any illegal material of this kind, but a
watchdog group spotted pornographic material on sites serviced
by CompuServe in Germany and the Bavarian court held that the
service provider was responsible. Accordingly, it found against
Somm. This decision, not surprisingly, was much criticized because even the prosecution had accepted that Somm himself was
innocent of the relevant offence and the defence claimed, with
considerable justification, that it was as unreasonable to prosecute
an ISP as to prosecute telephone companies for the content of
their customers' conversations, or to prosecute airlines for the
drugs some of their passengers smuggle.

The evident injustice of convicting the innocent for the crimes of others, of which this seems to be an instance, is one of the factors that makes the main alternative to licensing – labelling – more attractive. Labelling would apply directly to material that appears on the Internet rather than to the infrastructure which it employs. Again, there are systems something like this already in existence and we can use our experience of these to make more informed and less speculative guesses about how labelling might work. Take the system of classifying films which operates in some countries. Each new film or commercially produced video is given a certificate signifying its suitability for different viewing publics and a movie which is denied a certificate is thereby prevented from securing public viewing at all. There are several important points to be made about such systems of classification, but some of them relate more directly to the topic of the next section. For the moment, it is enough to observe that classification can take one of three forms. First, there is what is known as 'white listing'. Under such a system, nothing is permitted unless it carries a 'white' or approved label. Second, there is 'black listing' where everything is permitted unless it is labelled 'black'. Third, there is 'multi-coloured' listing, by which everything is given a 'colour' which advertises its character in advance. (This is consistent with the label 'black' leading to a ban, of course.)

Technically it is possible to incorporate devices which 'screen' according to 'colour' so that an individual computer (or television) is able to display only those items which have labels of a certain colour. Such devices tend to commend themselves to anxious parents because, in theory, they make it possible to restrict the sort of material that children can access while unsupervised. Translating the idea of this (or even the relatively simpler systems of 'black' and 'white') into a practical reality faces enormous and arguably insurmountable difficulties, however. This is because both 'white listing' and 'multi-coloured listing' requires prior scrutiny of all the material available on the Net. This is an impossible task. It is both impossible in the abstract and under the real conditions now prevailing. There is no theoretical limit to the amount of material which can make its way on to the Internet and it may thus be expected to exceed anything that could be scrutinized, but in any case there is *already* on the Internet an amount of material that is unsurveyable in anything but a random fashion, and the amount being added every day is huge. The position with 'black listing' is a little different because it only aims to exclude what we may assume to be small proportion of the total amount of accessible material. This is still a daunting task, but there is some reason for would-be 'black listers' to hope that such material might be 'caught' under general categories.

How might screening according to general categories of 'black' and 'white' be effected? One suggestion makes use of the existing technology of 'search engines'. 'Gophers' and other search engines are programs which scan material on the Internet and select according to some subject matter. Their normal use is for research of various kinds, not necessarily academic, in which the user gets the computer to range over very large amounts of material seeking only that which has some feature (often a 'key' word) to which the search engine then gives admission. Search engines can be fairly sophisticated and we may expect that they will become much more sophisticated yet. The motivating force behind them is the need to sort through huge amounts of material for specific purposes and, in essence, search engines simply extend the design and scope of the bibliographic indices which are a common feature of modern libraries. Without some such systematic scanning, whether in libraries or on the Internet, the material currently available is unmanageable and hence useless.

It is not difficult to imagine ways in which this device could be used for purposes of regulation. We only have to devise a sufficiently large and interrelated set of features, including source as well as content, and install it at ISP level to ensure that only material which passes scrutiny is accessible to users of that ISP. For example, we might build in a 'screen' that restricted access to material coming from public institutions and excluded everything that came from a private source. Even then, however, we may expect the system to be imperfect because some users in public institutions can be expected to abuse the systems within which they work for corrupt and nefarious purposes. Such a system would in effect blacklist everything it did not admit, but even on the most favourable scenario some material which it intended to blacklist would get through.

In my view, general category blacklisting combined in some way with licences requiring content management on the part of ISPs is the most practical suggestion to date for policing the Internet, and yet there is good reason to think that it would be largely ineffectual. This is for a number of reasons. First, as we have seen, any system of control will be less than perfect. For systems which aim to regulate very large numbers of individuals engaged in pursuits that are popular and (largely) private the degree of imperfection in their operation is likely to be great. Consider, by way of comparison but also by way of evidence, the international effort to control the use and trade in illegal drugs. Somewhat unusually, there is a very high degree of international consensus and cooperation with respect to drug control, and many governments (especially in the West) have devoted huge resources to its implementation. Nor is it without its successes. Each year sees the identification of sources, the seizure of very large quantities of drugs and the smashing of drug rings. Despite this, all the evidence suggests that the war on drugs is being lost, if by that we mean that drugtaking and trafficking have risen steadily during the very period of the war. We have no reason to think that the position would be any different with the policing of illicit material on the Internet. In fact, there is reason to think that it would be worse partly because material on the Internet is far harder to detect and to 'seize', and partly because it has begun life as an international system largely beyond the control of governments either singly or in concert.

A second important fact is that the system described as most practicable – 'black listing via ISPs' – is at its most practicable when it is voluntary. The anxious parents alluded to earlier are *seeking* ways in which to screen and one can imagine commercial service providers making the existence of such screening devices a selling point. But to move from this to the compulsory installation of such devices by law, is to bring into play a quite different set of considerations. This would require considerable political will within each jurisdiction and concerted international action on legislation and enforcement. The prospect of either, especially given the experience of trying to control drugs, is remote.

A third point relates more directly to the peculiarities of the Internet itself. To police it with any hope of effectiveness we would need to go beyond the crude physical measure of taking machines away and instead employ software devices. The trouble with this, however, is that the invention of every such device provides a stimulus to the invention of another device which will circumvent it. Once again we have some evidence to go on here. Computer hacking and computer viruses are a familiar part of information technology. In response to them much time and effort has been given to the invention of tighter security systems and to software vaccines. Many of these have been effective, but usually only for a time because the 'hackers', 'crackers' and 'phreakers' are no less skilled or dedicated than those who try to combat them. The result is a sort of cat-and-mouse relationship in which neither is wholly successful against the other. There is every reason to believe, in my view, that a similar fate would befall attempts to introduce content-management controls. Moreover, as in the case of drugs, there would be a powerful economic incentive at work. People would pay to secure access to the illicit material which the law tried to deny them, and this would both stimulate and feed the supply of programmers able and willing to try to subvert the controls. We need not be over-gloomy about the end result to see that, combined with the inevitable slack which there must be in the regulation of the Internet anyway, the outcome would almost certainly be the expenditure of very considerable amounts of public money in the cause of a war that can never be won and whose limited victories would in any case be temporary.

A final point worth making is this: it is not only unsavoury or crudely economic motives that would stimulate the relatively expert to try to subvert the system. Information technology is used, mostly, as a medium of expression and so the belief in free speech as the right of the individual would also be called into question, and would find its defenders. Indeed, already it is the case that suggestions about the need to police the Internet are strenuously opposed from many sides by those who believe in freedom, and in this connection we should add the further observation that, for long-standing cultural reasons, the belief in free speech is likely to find its strongest supporters in the United States, where the technology and the use of the Internet is at its most advanced.

This last point, in fact, provides a bridge with the next section. Those who incline to the view that the Internet needs policing assume that a sizeable amount of the material that is to be found there *ought* to be suppressed, and that it is both the right and the duty of the law to do so. It is against the background of some such assumption that the moral anarchy of the Internet is usually thought to constitute a problem (though this is not the ground I advanced in the last chapter) and only in the light of the same assumption that the very great practical difficulties we have uncovered in this section are grounds for pessimism. It is time, therefore, to turn to its examination.

The morality of pornography

The Internet contains harmful and pornographic material. We began with this assertion and nothing in the course of the argument has suggested anything to the contrary. Nor do I propose to deny it, because the more interesting moral, and philosophical, question is whether, if it is a fact, this implies that something should be done about it. It is a question that falls into two parts. Does the existence of such material on the Internet carry any moral implications for action and, if it does, do these in their turn carry any implications for the law? In this section we will be concerned with the moral dimension and in the next with the legal.

The existence of *harmful* material on the Internet is reasonably easily dealt with. As I observed earlier, in so far as what is on the Internet takes the form of written or graphic material, strictly speaking it is more accurately described as potentially rather than actually harmful, and arguably the position is not different to that of other media. If someone learns from the Internet how to make a bomb, this new knowledge in itself is not harmful to others; it only becomes so when they make the bomb (or even try to, perhaps). A more immediate kind of harm might be thought to reside in material that is defamatory or plagiarized. Here the harm done (if any) is done by the writing itself and not by some subsequent action. Even so, there is no reason to think that we are facing any-thing especially novel in such cases. Defamation and plagiarism are morally wrong on the Internet if they are morally wrong in books or newspapers, and in so far as there is reason to take legal steps against them in the older more familiar contexts there is rea-son to do so in this new context also. The medium of the Internet itself makes little difference. In fact the laws relating to libel, copy-right and even pornography can be and have been extended to en-compass the Internet without any great difficulty, either political or legal. The UK Defamation Act of 1996 extends existing legisla-tion to the Internet by treating ISPs as 'publishers', thus giving them the same legal responsibilities and liabilities as publishers of print. It is true that there are complications here (relating to objec-tions that arose in the Somm case), but the passing of this Act il-lustrates the general principle that the Internet does not necessarily throw up any *legal* novelties. It may be that acts of defamation and so on are harder to uncover on the Internet than they are in print. This is not a difference in kind however, and there may not even be all that much difference in degree. It is worth remembering that the amount of printed material in the world is also vast. In Britain alone the number of new titles pub-lished in one year has come close to 100,000 and it is highly likely that such a huge number of pages contains libellous and plagia-rized material which has gone undetected.

A similar point can be made about computer theft and fraud. These too can be more directly harmful than the bombmaking case because to have the computer record of your wealth reduced can be indistinguishable from having your wealth reduced. But these offences are subject to just the same moral strictures and le-gal remedies that they are in the world at large. Detection and prosecution of computer theft and fraud may be more difficult, but this does not make the moral or legal parameters either more complex or more interesting.

There is more to be said about harm and the law, but I am in-clined to think that the existence of harmful (as opposed to poten-tially harmful) material on the Internet raises no specially new normative issues. This may explain why people seem to be more concerned about pornography, and regard the scope the Internet gives to paedophiles and the like as more insidious than the advantages it lends to relatively 'ordinary' crooks and criminals.

But what exactly *is* pornography and why is it objectionable? A very great deal has been written on the subject and it is obviously an issue that applies to many other media besides the Internet – books, magazines, video tapes, films and photographs, for example. So in addition to examining the nature of pornography in general, we will need to bear in mind what, if anything, can be said about the peculiarities of the Internet as a medium for it. The dictionary defines pornography as 'the obscene in painting, writing, film and the like'. It defines the obscene as 'offensive to the senses or sensibilities'. The legal definition by contrast with the dictionary definition has tended to characterize obscenity in terms of its consequences, most notably in the celebrated phrase 'having a tendency to deprave and corrupt'. The trouble with both styles of definition is that they appear to go round in something like a circle because they employ terms in the *definiens* about which there might be as much unclarity and dispute as the *definiendum*. If we can ask the question 'Just what *is* pornography?', it seems we can no less easily ask 'Just what *is* offensive or depraved or corrupting?'. To define the former in terms of the latter, therefore, is to be no further forward.

We do not need to break this circle, however, to make some headway with the argument. Take for instance the dictionary's appeal to 'offending senses and sensibilities'. Whatever we mean by this exactly, it is plain that my senses and sensibilities can only be offended if they have been exposed to the offending material. This immediately throws some additional light on the subject. First, pornography characterized in this way cannot exist in and of itself but only in so far as it is perceived. Second, its pornographic nature depends to some extent on the mind of those who perceive it – a small child can look at a picture without being aware of or susceptible to its salacious character, for instance. From these two observations it follows that pornography is problematic only *in relation*. I cannot be offended by that which I do not see or read. It follows that each individual has the opportunity to render the effects of pornography null and void, by ignoring it. In this, the pornographic is to be sharply distinguished from the harmful. The

negative character of harms and injuries cannot be avoided by being ignored.

Now it can be argued with respect to some media that ignoring
pornographic material is easier said than done. Billboards and
public broadcasting stations intrude upon the public willy-nilly (or
at least they can) and sometimes this is true of bookstalls also. Let
us agree that this is so, but if it is, it makes pornography on the
Internet of *less* concern than pornography elsewhere. There may
be a vast amount of pornographic material there if I choose to
surf for it, but if I choose not to, my senses and sensibilities will
remain unscathed.

A second point arises from the essential subjectivity of pornography, though to appreciate it we need to be clear about what subjectivity means here. What it does *not* mean is that the *badness* of
pornography is subjective – wrong, that is to say, only in virtue of
our thinking it wrong. The inclination to assume this nowadays is
widespread, partly because people differ rather greatly in their attitudes to pornography and partly because moral subjectivism in
general is a commonly held view. Whatever the truth about moral
subjectivism, however, it is quite consistent to hold both that
pornographic depictions of sex and violence, and a love of them,
are objectively evil and at the same time that their effect is (in the
words of the *Book of Common Prayer*) their ability 'to assault and
hurt the soul'. What this compelling phrase expresses is the idea
that the principal impact of indulging in certain sorts of fantasy is
on states of mind and character, and that this is bad in itself irrespective of what actions may or may not flow from it. It is in this
sense that pornography is *essentially* subjective, a matter of purity
and impurity of *mind* rather than rightness or wrongness of deed.

That there is some such distinction to be drawn seems to me
difficult to deny. There is a very strong tendency in the modern
world to hold that the value of states of mind and character,
whether good or bad, resides entirely in the outward actions these
give rise to. Accordingly, there is a corresponding tendency to ignore the essentially subjective character of pornography and discuss its rights and wrongs solely in terms of the objective harms it
causes or is alleged to cause. But we can easily imagine the case of
someone who, say, spends a great deal of time finding and perus-

ing very lurid child pornography but never commits any overt act against a child. In terms of outward effects their interest is harmless and for this reason many people would wonder whether there is 'really' anything wrong about it. Yet most of these same people, I contend, would be ashamed to admit to the fact if they shared this person's interest. To list 'child pornography' as among one's interests in *Who's Who* or some similar publication is unthinkable for most people, and to have it come out inadvertently that this is in fact one of the ways in which one spends one's leisure time is a cause for embarrassment and shame. If the only mark of moral wrong is the causing of outward harm, however, what is there to be ashamed of? The answer is nothing. Since there *is* something to be ashamed of, it follows that causing outward harm cannot be the only mark of moral wrong. What else might it be? The answer is that the revelation shows up a state of mind and character which is sordid, whether or not it leads to the injuring or alarming of others.

In older language, there are gross appetites and interests. People can resist them, fail to do so or wilfully indulge them. Which they do is relevant to moral character, just as whether people's thoughts about others are charitable or uncharitable, contemptuous or sympathetic, are morally relevant facts even if their outward treatment does not specially reflect these attitudes. Indeed, it can be the case that someone disguises their contempt or loathing for the sake of personal advantage, in which case their moral fault is compounded by deception. Those who deny these claims about moral relevance and focus exclusively on causing harm (or doing good) to others as the sole criterion of moral rectitude seem to me to fly in the face of obvious fact. They are also committed to discounting entirely as moral the themes which countless poets, playwrights and novelists have explored with great subtlety and imagination.

There is a case for saying, then, that pornography matters morally whether or not it leads to the social harms that many allege. People resist this conclusion sometimes because they fear that it implies intrusion into the private lives of others. If people want to engage in orgiastic fantasies of a perverted kind in the privacy of their own minds, what is that to me and who am I to interfere?

Such a response, as it seems to me, indicates another important presupposition of contemporary thinking – that the moral is relevant only in so far as it implies some course of conduct. But why should this be so? There are many vices – hypocrisy, meanness, narrow-mindedness – which we may see all too clearly in others and about which there is nothing to be done. That there is nothing to be *done* about them, however, does not mean that they do not exist or are of no moral significance. To suppose that it does, is to assume an action-directed conception of morality which, if common in the contemporary discussion of these issues, is both a distortion and an aberration peculiar to the modern period. Conversely, there are virtues which we see in others – generosity, tolerance, the ability to forgive – about which there is also nothing to do, except admire and hope to find them reflected in ourselves.

What is true is that these virtues and vices do not spring up out of the blue any more than other meritorious attributes do. For example, the ability to write English with both lucidity and style is a gift which many, however hard they try, will never emulate and can only admire. But it is not purely innate: it is made possible only within the context of a long tradition of language and literature. Good writing promotes good writing – not invariably and inevitably it is true, but the connection is nonetheless clear for all that. So too with moral virtues. These are not 'in-born' in the way that blue eyes or brown hair are. They arise within a social and historical context, and their possibility is handed on by means of moral traditions. Such traditions can undergo corruption and collapse, and it is the possibility of corruption and the fear of collapse that sustain the view elaborated in the last chapter that there is some reason to regard the Internet as an instrument of moral anarchy. If, as I have now been arguing, an important part of morality is concerned more with judgement than with action – what to *think* rather than what to *do* – this leaves us with a question about whether the moral anarchy of the Internet calls for any practical programme of action and, if so, what. It is a topic to which we will return in the next chapter.

For present purposes, this much is certain. Character and the moral standards by which it is assessed are not primarily concerned with *acting* but with *being*. To suppose that the two are wholly divorced would also be a mistake, of course. People whose motives are bad frequently act in ways that are injurious to others. On the other hand, people may also harm others from the best of intentions. Either way, social life depends in part upon the regulation of action. This is the point, arguably, at which morality must be supplemented by legality.

Pornography and legality

I have been defending the claim that morality is mistakenly construed if it is thought of primarily as a matter of bringing benefits or causing harm to others. Over a wide range of cases in fact, moral judgement and assessment are much more concerned with states of mind and character – what earlier periods called 'the soul'. This explains why, though there may well be reason to be concerned about the moral impact of pornography on the Internet, it does not follow that such concern warrants the invocation of law. Indeed, there is something absurd about the idea that one could legislate for moral virtue or against moral vice. Could we really have laws that required us to be kind, generous or hospitable, and forbade us to be cowardly, vengeful or mean-spirited? I take these to be rhetorical questions: their answer, in the negative, is obvious.

Nevertheless, there is certainly reason to be concerned about the harm some people do to others. If this is a moral matter, it is a moral matter in which the law can reasonably interest itself. In fact, there is a venerable tradition with this as its leading thought, expressed most famously in John Stuart Mill's essay *On Liberty*.

> The object of this Essay is to assert one very simple principle, as entitled to govern absolutely the dealings of society with the individual in the way of compulsion and control, whether the means used be physical force in the form of legal penalties, or the moral coercion of public opinion. That principle is, that the sole end for which mankind are warranted, individually or collectively, in interfering with the liberty of action of any of their number, is self-protection. That the only purpose for which power can rightfully be exercised over any member of a

civilized community, against his will, is to prevent harm to others. His own good, either physical or moral, is not a sufficient warrant.

(Mill, pp. 14–15)

This is a principle that has commended itself to many, as being *obviously* sensible. At the time of its publication, though, it was regarded as highly contentious and, despite its obviousness to the modern mind, there are indeed good reasons to regard it as problematic. Let us disregard these for the moment, however, and apply Mill's principle to pornography. One crucial question is this: does pornography actually cause harm? In the last section I argued that this is not the central issue when it comes to considering the morality or immorality of pornography, but if Mill is right it *is* the central question when we consider what attitude the law should take to it.

The question 'Does pornography cause harm?' is not a philosophical or a moral question, but an empirical one. No one, I think, denies this, but what many do deny is that it is a question needing special scientific investigation. It stands to reason, they will say, that the more violence there is displayed on our television and computer screens, whether fictional or actual, the more there will be in our streets. When pressed for evidence, some have even argued that the connection is so obvious that no evidence is needed. Now there are long-standing and widely accepted philosophical arguments which show that a factual proposition cannot be self-evident in the strict sense. Add to this the observation that people in the past have often been mistaken about what is 'obvious' and it seems clear that any claim about the effects of pornography can only be made good by adducing real evidence for it.

If this is accepted, however, the 'self-evident' connection evaporates. It appears to be the case that convincing evidence of the harmful effects of pornography is lacking. No substantial study to date has established a clear statistical, still less causal, connection. What tends to generate and sustain a belief in the harmfulness of pornography are the high-profile cases reported in the press and on television. However, even the seemingly plainest and most telling instances cannot clinch the matter. This is because the theories of psychological motivation with which they must ultimately be supported allow interpretation in different directions. The most compelling examples usually cited are 'copycat crimes' – killings or acts of violence which appear to replicate the details of some 'video nasty' – and we can readily imagine the same sort of example being connected with material on the Internet. But as far as the facts go, it is just as plausible to think that the connection between the two is *not* cause and effect. It may be rather that the psychology of someone who is fascinated by such images is also the psychology of a violent or murderous person. To decide between this explanation of the connection – that both have the same underlying cause – and the more common contention – that the first is the cause of the second – we need hard evidence about patterns of crime, the motivations of actual criminals and the psychological basis of antisocial behaviour. Nothing in this matter 'stands to reason' and we do not have this hard evidence. What we do know, from a number of studies, is that the mentality of most multiple murderers, child-molesters and the very violent is complex and extremely hard to understand, if indeed it is intelligible at all. For this reason it is naive to imagine that we can estimate the contribution that watching pornographic videos or spending too much time on the Internet might make to the balance of forces within such minds. In short, even in the case of what appears to be the most straightforward of copycat crimes we cannot attribute any clear causal weight to any act of viewing or reading which preceded it. There is no more reason to think that this was the cause of the deranged state than that it is simply more evidence of it.

Violence does beget violence, it seems to me, but we ought not to confuse this with a quite different thesis – that the *depiction* of violence (factual or fictional) begets violence. This is a more ambitious thesis and correspondingly harder to establish. The world before radio, television, full-colour magazines or the Internet was not lacking in cruelty and violence, and a great deal of present-day violence does not seem importantly connected with modern media. Some of the most frightful carnage this century – Cambodia's killing fields or the civil strife in Rwanda, for example – has taken place in societies where television, videos and the Internet are almost unknown.

One response to this scepticism about the power of the pornographic to cause harm might be a counsel of caution. We may not *know* that violent and perverted images do give rise to violence and perversion, but why not prefer caution to licence? Such caution is not without price, however. Every legal proscription brings a corresponding cost – a cost in terms of the liberty of other citizens and a cost in terms of the resources which must be devoted to applying the law. Earlier in this chapter we reviewed some of the major practical difficulties which lie in the way of effective policing of the Internet, difficulties that are mirrored to some extent in the enforcement of laws relating to drugs. In those countries where the law has been invoked against pornography, the record of success in applying it is not much better and in many cases has proved counter-productive. Material that is banned tends to attract far greater attention and be much more sought after than if it had never been banned in the first place. Such bans also raise a difficulty which the argument of earlier sections promised to return to, namely the legal definition of pornography.

There are at least three major problems facing the legal definition of pornography. The first is that any attempt to define it in terms of effects – such as the traditional British test of 'tending to deprave and corrupt' – rest on empirical contentions which, as we have seen, are as yet without substantial foundation. Second, to rely on the alternative test of 'offending sensibilities' is to make the law subject to changing patterns of public opinion. Material which could be guaranteed to offend sensibilities twenty or thirty years ago can now be found on prime-time television. This introduces an important injustice in the application of the law because it means that people are treated differently, not because they have done different things, but merely because they have done the same thing at different times. Third, there is a close connection between pornography and purpose. That is to say, the same material can figure in quite different sorts of activity. For example, in 1998 a British student took photographs to a commercial laboratory to be developed. When the developer saw the pictures, he reported the student to the police. They then seized the photographs, tracked down the original book from which they had been copied and sought to have it destroyed. All this was done on the basis of the content of the photographs. However, the student was in fact engaged in a study of the work of the American artist and photographer Robert Mapplethorpe, and had borrowed the book from a university library and copied the photographs for the purposes of a dissertation. We do not need to go into the question of whether Mapplethorpe's originals were art or pornography (though this is an importantly relevant question) in order to see that the *student* was not engaged in producing or disseminating pornography, even though it could well be the case that the photographs in question would pass the test of offending sensibilities. Conversely, it is possible to imagine cases where material which would strike most people as relatively innocent is circulated secretly for lascivious purposes. (This sometimes happens among small children, in fact, who can have an amusingly innocent idea of what is 'naughty'.) In short, it is not possible to define pornography for legal or any other purposes in terms of content. But if this is not possible, we cannot expect to police the Internet, or any other medium, with an eye to what is found there.

So far then the case for making pornography subject to regulation by the criminal law is weak. Yet another objection arises if we raise a more radical question: is there good reason to accept Mill's harm principle anyway? Preventing harm to others strikes many people as an eminently sensible test by which determine what should and should not be included in a criminal code, but despite this there are a number of rather obvious objections. Is the principle supposed to lay down a necessary or a sufficient condition for making something against the law? That is to say, is the fact that an action is harmful to other people *one* condition that must be satisfied if it is to be justifiably proscribed by law, or is this fact the *only* condition that needs to be satisfied? Whichever interpretation we give it, and together they seem to exhaust the possibilities, it is easy to think of actions which do not fit either but about which a free society ought to take a different view. There are rights – privacy, for instance – the violation of which may cause no harm in any straightforward sense. Peeping Toms and stalkers may cause fear and alarm, but even if they do not, the people they watch can reasonably claim a right to privacy. To make the causing of harm a necessary condition of proscription would thus require the law to permit the violation of such rights. If, on the other hand, we interpret Mill's principle in terms of sufficiency then another class of actions presents difficulties. There are harmful actions – successful commercial competition is one example – which it would be highly detrimental to ordinary life to make illegal. Economic protectionism is an attempt to prevent the harm that free trade does to vested interests, but the mere fact that it is aimed at preventing such harm does not obviously make it acceptable or justifiable. This implication is specially ironic since Mill's harm condition was originally advanced in the more general context of economic *laissez-faire*.

There seems good reason, then, not merely to doubt the empirical claim that pornography causes harm, but to question the underlying presupposition that, if it does, there is sufficient warrant for its legal proscription or control. Once we add these conclusions to the conclusions of former sections, the case *against* policing the Internet appears to be as conclusive as arguments of this sort can be. It may be summarized as follows.

First, there is the question of practicability. We saw that this is not just a matter of the availability of technological means. Given the nature of the Internet there are certainly technical obstacles to effective policing, but in themselves these might be overcome. Once set in the wider context of political possibility, international relations and the deployment of government resources, however, the practicality of policing the Net fades dramatically. This should worry us only if there is reason to be concerned about some of the material that the Internet may be used to produce and disseminate. More obviously harmful material – recipes for bomb-making and the like – is certainly a cause for concern, but so it is in other media and there is no reason to think that the Internet presents us with special novelties to which existing forms of control cannot be applied. The case of pornography is different, but while there is some ground for moral concern about this, a proper understanding of morality suggests that the root of the concern lies not in socially harmful actions but in the possible corruption of mind and character. Allowing nonetheless that such corruption can lead to action, there is indeed reason to consider the suggestion that the law has a role here – setting limits on the excesses which will cause harm. But at the same time this suggestion rests upon two suppositions that there is reason to doubt – namely, that there is an establishable causal connection between pornography and harmful action, and that the causing of harm is in itself a sufficient warrant for legal restriction. Neither of these contentions can be sustained. We may conclude, therefore, that there is no role for the law with respect to the Internet other than the role it plays, and has played for a long time in other media, with respect to copyright, fraud, libel, theft of intellectual property and so on.

How can we rest content with such a negative outcome given the arguments in Chapter 5? For these showed that there is some substance to the fear that the Internet is an instrument of moral anarchy. To address this issue we ought to remind ourselves that the only real ground for anxiety is a moral one, and that this relates primarily not to the question of what people might be doing to one another, but what sort of people they are becoming. The fear which the advent of the Internet plausibly induces lies not so much in the prospect of lawlessness, but in worthlessness. It is a fear captured, in part, in the title of one of Neil Postman's books, referred to at an earlier stage: *Amusing Ourselves to Death*. Is this the sort of people and the sort of society we want to become? At this point a further range of issues is raised. Is the Internet to be regarded as merely an extension, and probably a corruption, of society as we know it, or does it present the possibility of new forms of society and community? Luddites will focus on the negative social aspects of the Internet; Technophiles will stress the positive social advances it promises. Which of them is right? This is the topic of the next chapter.

7   New communities

Is the Internet merely a dissolution of society as we know it, or does it have the makings of wholly new social forms? Those who take the gloomy view are open to an important objection: why pin the responsibility for further social fragmentation on the Internet? In so far as it is intensifying a descent into moral anarchy, the fault lies not with the Internet as such, but with the society and culture out of which it has sprung. While it is not implausible to argue that the Internet provides greater scope to radical individualism, individualism itself is the product of social changes far wider and more long-standing than anything the Internet has, or could have, accomplished.

Individuals, communities and interest groups

With this rejoinder to the Neo-Luddite, we touch upon a subject which has been the stock-in-trade of both sociology and political philosophy for several decades. Sociologists have for some time been gathering evidence of the decline and disintegration of social organizations and the growth of widespread political alienation, most notably in the United States (where, after all, the Internet began and is most widely used). The body of evidence is too large to rehearse, still less review here, but we may usefully point to some of its most salient conclusions. Chief among these is the decline of the traditional family unit. The advent of effective birth control, the relative ease and dramatic increase of divorce, the consequent rise in one-parent families and single-person households, are interrelated changes that have intensified each other to the point where in some parts of some US cities, the traditional family – two parents presiding over their children's only home – is in a small minority. Second, in turn this change (it is claimed) has given rise to a steep fall in membership of voluntary associations, a fall variously calculated at between 25 per cent and 50 per cent since mid-century. Third, this tendency is exacerbated by higher levels of education and prosperity which have led to greater labour mobility and thus to the breaking of family and other social ties by geographical dispersal. In both birth and adulthood, upbringing and expectation, individuals are floating freer and freer of the familial and communal ties which formerly bound them.

What is true of the United States has been found to be true in Western Europe also and, since the rest of the world in the twentieth century has followed the US in so many things, we may expect that even where fragmentation is less marked at present, it will become more so in the future. This displacement of social groups by individual agents has a more alarming side than the mere collapse of worthy voluntary organizations. Those who have studied the enormous increase in the incidence of multiple murderers have gradually come out against psychological explanations and turned to explanations of a more sociological kind. As Elliot Leyton puts it: 'if the killers are merely insane, why do they in fact so rarely display the cluster of identifiable clinical symptoms ... which psychiatrists agree mark mental illness?' It seems more likely, though difficult to show, that in such a phenomenon we are seeing evidence of deep social change, a radical shift from community to individual as the focus of ordinary life with a consequent rise in radically alienated 'loners' – a suggestion that several in-depth studies of particular cases have done something to bear out.

What is the basic cause of this fragmentation? One relatively banal explanation is the invention and rapid spread of television, for it seems to be the case that by a very wide margin the most common pastime of most people in developed countries nowadays is watching television – a private, non-social (some would say anti-social) activity. Yet we can hardly rest content with this as the primary explanation, since it seems plausible to hold that the popularity of television is at least as much a symptom as a cause of the decline of more communal activity. Moreover, if this is all that there were to be said, we should not have evidence for much more than a change in tastes and leisure pursuits. In fact, there is a danger that too much is read into social trends. Robert D. Puttnam has observed, for example, that while the total number of bowlers in the United States increased by 10 per cent in the period 1980–93, league bowling decreased by 40 per cent – he has read into this a 'Strange Disappearance of Social Capital in America', the subtitle of his original essay on this theme. But whatever the strength of his contention, the fact in itself is consistent with a simple and more superficial explanation: changing fashion.

Still, there does appear to be more than fashion at work. In a well-received study by Robert Bellah and others, *Habits of the Heart*, the phenomenon of communal disintegration (in the United States) was to some degree confirmed when Bellah and his co-authors found a serious decline in social networks – churches, clubs, trade unions and so on – which formerly enabled participants to work together for shared objectives. They went on to hypothesize a connection between this decline and the demise of shared religious and moral outlooks. In my terminology, they postulated an underlying growth of moral anarchy which, by undermining the *meaningfulness* of communal participation, thereby eroded it. Whether the empirical evidence can really be made to bear out such an hypothesis is a large and very difficult question, partly because it raises the even larger (and yet more long-standing) subject of secularization – that radical shift from religious to non-religious conceptions of life and its value which social theorists have claimed to detect at least since Friedrich Engels in the 1840s. But the very fact that such a claim can be advanced with some credibility connects the investigations of contemporary sociology with one of the dominant themes of recent political philosophy and hence with the topics of this book. This is the debate between liberalism and communitarianism.

The liberal versus communitarian debate concerns not empirical data about changing social patterns but the fundamental philosophical ideas which underlie rival conceptions of social life. The debate does not consist in a single issue, however, but in an interconnected set of issues, some (though not all) of which have to do with the relation between the individual and the community. While within this debate the term 'community' has played a part, most versions of what is known as 'communitarianism' do not in fact make much use of the term community itself. It is true that liberalism, in most of its varieties, can be construed as a social doctrine that does indeed assign a central place to the individual. It is also true that there is a philosophically important contrast to be drawn between individuals and communities. Nevertheless, it is not the case that communitarianism is equally well characterized as a doctrine that gives a central moral role to the community. Indeed, there is something to be said for the contention that communitarianism is not a positive social doctrine at all, but simply the negation of liberal individualism, and the grounds on which liberalism is rejected differ, as it seems to me, according to different versions of communitarianism. There is also good reason to hold that the central point at issue between these two philosophical positions, at least as they have been elaborated in modern political philosophy, is not the relative priority of the community and the individual, but the relative priority of 'the right' and 'the good' – between, that is to say, principles of social organization and the values of a human life.

These are matters to be returned to shortly, but it is worth observing that outside philosophy – in the worlds of ideas and affairs – 'community' has become a vogue word on almost every lip, a word now used, or abused, to the point of meaninglessness. As a result it has lost such descriptive precision as it once had and retains only a faintly positive 'buzz'. It is possible, if common usage is any indication, to belong to the local community, the gay community, the scientific community, the business community, the rural community and even the international community, all at once. In fact, it seems that we cannot fail to be members of some community or other. But if so, this only shows that communal membership means nothing.

What connection is there between these vague uses of the word in popular parlance, and the philosophical disputes that invoke the language of communitarianism? And what connection is there between the philosophical debate, the findings of sociologists and the concerns of social policy-makers? We can only answer these questions if we first clear the ground of foggy terminology. This requires us to establish a more precise sense for the idea of a community, not by *discovering* what its 'real' sense is, but by *giving* it a sense which will enable it to do some useful and substantial intellectual work.

We can begin this task by noting one context in which limited but relatively precise use is still made of the term. This is in the phrase 'religious community'. To those who are using the description accurately, a religious community is not just any religious organization – it is not a congregation, a denomination, a church or a parish, for instance – but a body organized according to a set of highly specific rules for communal living and shared activity, and to which individuals are admitted after a noviciate. The most obvious examples are convents and monasteries, and though there are other religious communities too, it is these I shall take as exemplars. Just what feature of a convent or monastery makes it a community is something to be considered further, but it should be clear that however we characterize them, they can be contrasted with communities in the current commonplace use. Neither the gay community nor the business community, still less the international community, is or could be a community in this sense.

In the first two of these phrases (in my view the third is too grandiose to make any sense of) what is being conceived of as a unity is really a grouping of interests – a body of individuals who are bound together not by any constituting principle, but by the contingent fact of having interests in common. It is what Bellah and his co-authors refer to as an 'enclave' – a term they contrast with 'community', and one which I shall use. We should notice that the phrase 'interest group' is ambiguous: it can mean a group of individuals who are interested in the same things, or a group of individuals whose material, economic or other interests coincide. In the first sense, stamp-collectors and train-spotters are interest groups; in the second sense, farmers and stockbrokers are.

These two senses of interest group are not extensionally exclusive, of course. People who are interested in the same things may also find that the same things are in their interest – that is, to their benefit or disadvantage – and where the two coincide we have what, following Bellah, I shall call an 'enclave'. The advantage of this semi-technical term is that it gives us a name for the fairly common co-extension of what are conceptually distinct senses of interest, while providing a contrast with a third conception, community proper. All three – interest group, enclave and community – are distinguishable concepts which it is important to record but which the common use of 'community' often serves to confound. I shall mark the difference between the two senses of interest which together comprise an 'enclave' by distinguishing between a 'subjective interest group' and an 'objective interest group'. A *subjective* interest group is a grouping whose members happen to be interested in the same things. An *objective* interest group is one whose members are, as a matter of fact, beneficially or adversely affected by the same things.

An enclave, then, is a set of people forming an interest group in both senses. It is, we might say, bound by feeling and by fact. What is the difference between such an enclave and a community properly so-called? There is at least one feature we can isolate which is missing from an enclave but present in a community, at least if we take the idea of a religious community as our guide. A convent, for example, is composed of people interested in the same things – the worship of God and the nursing of the terminally ill, let us say. It is also true that objectively the same things stand to affect them – government health policy or the law on freedom of religion, for example. But even the combination of both subjective and objective interest is insufficient to constitute membership of the community, because it is plain that a religiously inclined nurse in a secular hospital would also be a member of both groups, but not, *ex hypothesi*, a member of the community in question.

The missing ingredient is this, I think. Members of the community properly so-called are subject to a Rule, and this Rule determines both what their objective interests *are* and what their subjective interests *ought to be*. Both determinations are achieved in part by the content of the Rule itself and in part by an office whose authority itself derives from the authority of the Rule, an office known as the Superior – the Abbot in a monastery and the Mother Superior in a convent. To simplify the terminology, I shall say simply that the members of such a community are *essentially* and not merely *contingently* interrelated, or, to put the same point in other language, that their common identity *as* a community is defined by their owing obedience to a mutually recognized authority.

Suppose we grant that these three features – objective interest, subjective interest and defining authority together make up a community properly so-called. What else, apart from a religious community, might be described as a community proper? It is evident that most things that are called communities in the common speech of today lack one or more of the three characteristics. For instance, the gay community is a subjective interest group but it is not subject to a defining authority. More interestingly, it can be argued that the gay 'community' is not an objective interest group either because its members are not all beneficially or adversely affected by the same things. By contrast, the business community *is* an objective interest group. Possibly, though not necessarily, it is also a subjective one – it depends how we characterize subjective interest. Are those who manufacture guns and those who manufacture butter, at some level or other, interested in the same things? Whatever we say about this, it is clear that, though subject (like everything else) to law in general, the world of commerce and industry is subject to no *defining* authority: anyone who manages to trade to whatever end and by whatever means is engaged in business.

A more promising example of community proper beyond the monastery walls is to be found in the political community, where this expression refers to a single, identifiable legal jurisdiction and a sovereign state. The citizens of a polity form an objective interest group, which is why we can speak of 'the national interest', and moreover they can plausibly be said to be subject to a defining authority – the law. That is to say, there are discoverable rules and procedures by which membership of the political community is acknowledged, granted, withheld or denied. The *polis* is not a subjective interest group, however, and interestingly this puts a limit on the role of its defining authority. Parliament can determine who is to hold British citizenship, but unlike a religious community it cannot also determine what true Britons ought to be interested in, what they ought to believe in, or whether they are mean or generous in their dealings with others. Though it can legitimately take steps to counter subversion, it cannot even require that citizens believe in the continuing existence of Britain as a political entity. Individual Britons who seek the demise of the British state by its total integration into the European Union, for example, are entitled to work to this end provided that they do so lawfully.

The best contenders for a *non-religious* community, in my view, are tribal societies without governments such as the societies in East Africa studied by Evans-Pritchard and other anthropologists in the first part of this century, and which, importantly, provide illuminating models for anarchists (in the limited political sense) who are also communitarians – the political theorist Michael Taylor in his book *Community, Anarchy and Liberty* is a good example. These small, often nomadic, societies are noted for their highly integrated character and for the degree of control they exercise over their members. This ranges not only over conduct, we might say, but over character. Interestingly though, belonging to such a society is not a matter of legal or constitutional definition, because within them there is little in the way of law and nothing in the way of a constitution. Membership turns on the adoption and acceptance, usually by birth, of the practices, customs and beliefs of the tribe.

Such communal integration can be attractive to Western minds precisely because it stands in sharp contrast to the fragmentation and alienation whose problematic character we are examining. But it can be romanticized; it has a downside, which consists in the near total absence of what we in the West would regard as individuality. It may even be said to be antithetical to ordinary, relatively simple freedoms. In fact, though the example of these societies is not that which first springs to mind when the term is used, they are properly described as 'totalitarian'; membership of them, like membership of a religious community, brings with it an *essential* determination of subjective and objective interest, and is thus highly unconducive to the existence of 'free spirits'.

A crucial point to observe about the membership of such societies is that (by contrast to religious communities) in the main it is not voluntary: the individual is born into it. It is in this feature that the justification of their classification as 'totalitarian' is to be found. The rejection of political totalitarianism, in fact, can most simply be characterized as the rejection of any assumption that social membership by accident of birth should determine what the subjective interests ought to be of those who happen to find themselves the subjects of a particular *polis*. This way of putting the objection reveals the connection between anti-totalitarianism and opposition to any interdependence between the state and a church, a party or a moral cause. In a free society the laws we are justifiably subject to cannot require us to have the habits or convictions of a Catholic, a Marxist or a Nazi. It also reveals, at last, the connection between the analysis of the concept of community and contemporary debates about liberal individualism.

Liberalism versus communitarianism

The literature on the liberalism/communitarianism debate is vast. For those unfamiliar with it, a full treatment would have to be of a length impossible to contemplate in the present context. On the other hand, for those familiar with the debate, to go into this literature in detail would be to traverse yet again some very well-trodden ground. I propose, therefore, simply to highlight two central themes that have been discussed under this heading and which can be made to bear directly on the issues surrounding the Internet with which this chapter is concerned.

Modern versions of liberal political philosophy tend to follow the work of John Rawls whose book, *A Theory of Justice*, we have had occasion to note in an earlier chapter, pretty much set the whole agenda for political philosophy for two decades. Here, however, a different aspect of his work is relevant. Rawls's aim is to formulate the principles which underlie a free and just society, at least as this is exemplified in Western democracies. His strategy is to imagine a set of conditions (called the Original Position) under which rational self-interested agents are unencumbered by partial (in the sense of partisan) interests and allegiances. The task is then to determine what principles of social organization individuals in the Original Position could be expected to subscribe to. On the basis of this strategy he elaborates two such principles: one governing liberty of action and the other governing the distribution of goods and benefits. A large part of Rawls's own interest lies in tracing out the implications of these two principles and many others have followed him in this. But most critical attention has focused on the fundamental argumentative strategy behind these implications. In particular, critics generally grouped under the label 'communitarian' have argued that the deliberators he describes in the Original Position are incoherent fictions since, stripped of all their social allegiances and personal interests, individuals as such have no basis for deliberation at all. Forget that you are a woman, a descendant of slaves, a Jew or a Catholic, and you have forgotten who you are. Individuals, this criticism runs, are 'radically situated'. That is to say, their identity as agents rests on a world of ideas and values not of their choosing, but in which they simply find themselves.

The point is put with special clarity by Alasdair MacIntyre in *After Virtue*, a book no less influential in this debate than Rawls's *Theory of Justice*.

> From the standpoint of individualism I am what I myself choose to be. I can always, if I wish to, put in question what are taken to be merely contingent social features of my existence ... [but] the story of my life is always embedded in the story of those communities from which I derive my identity. I am born with a past; and to try to cut myself off from that past, in an individualist mode, is to deform my present relationships. The possession of an historical identity and the possession of a social identity coincide ... What I am, therefore, is in key part, what I inherit, a specific past that is present to some degree in my present. I find myself part of a history and that is generally to say, whether I like it or not, whether I recognize it or not, one of the bearers of a tradition.

(MacIntyre, pp. 205–6)

The world in which individuals are thus radically situated is the society to which they inevitably, and not by their own choosing, belong. Given the analysis of the previous section, this society must have the elements of a community. That is to say, it cannot consist in a mere confluence of the subjective interests individuals *qua* individuals happen to have, because there is no deeper foundation in which these interests could be rooted. It must, rather, provide the constituting basis of such interests. We are interested in those things we have learnt to be interested in and the necessity of such learning implies a world outside our own impulses and desires. To take a pedestrian but illuminating example: I may have individual preferences about cakes or wines, but these must range over the things I have discovered to be on offer at the baker's and the wine merchant's. I cannot have such preferences *de novo*, as it were. To take a more significant example: I have to decide what it is I think and what I shall say about this or that, but I do not have it in my power to constitute the language in which to say it. This language is a natural language, *my* natural language, and in learning it I learn not merely the means to self-expression, but standards and criteria which determine what things are worth saying.

If this is true, if individuals really are 'radically situated' in this sense and not radically autonomous as the device of the Original Position seems to require, then a second major aspect of the Rawlsian project must also be rejected. This is the priority of 'the right' over 'the good' – a doctrine mentioned briefly at an earlier point in the chapter. Rawls believes that a free and just society requires its citizens to distinguish sharply between those beliefs and values which they hold central to their conception of a worthwhile and valuable life on the one hand (the good), and those rules and principles of social coordination that they expect all members of their society to adhere to on the other (the right). He further contends that principles of social right must be given priority over the good in this sense: the principles by which a free society is structured and regulated must be neutral with respect to the (possible) conceptions of the good that their citizens endorse. The principles of a just society cannot 'privilege' any one conception of the good over any other.

This doctrine of political neutrality (already touched on at an earlier stage in the discussion) is a more abstract and ambitious version of an older belief in the separation of church and state, and a version of the traditional liberal claim that morality and law should not be confounded but held distinct. In all versions, but especially the modern abstract one, it is another aspect of liberalism from which communitarian critics dissent. The ground of their dissent is simply a further application of the objection to radical individualism. It can be expressed in several ways. Conceptions of the good underlie and shape individual choices and preferences. To commend or require a choice or a preference with respect to social organization and regulation, therefore, we must appeal to underlying values. But these values have to be part of the individual's conception of the good which is itself constituted by the community to which they belong. In what else could such values be grounded? If this is so, however, the idea that individuals in the Original Position can be divorced from such conceptions is incoherent and the requirement that individuals in real societies should adopt an attitude of neutrality with respect to them is nihilistic. That is to say, such neutrality would not provide values with an independent foundation but deprive them of any foundation at all. Alternatively, the communitarian criticism can be stated more simply as the view that the authority of law depends upon a shared morality. To require that it be neutral with respect to any and every morality is thus to deprive it of any authority. On what basis can it then commend itself?

I have set this dispute out in a way that may seem to favour the communitarian critic. Yet there are rejoinders to be made on Rawls's behalf, of course, some of which he has himself made in later works. To consider these, however, would necessitate entering into matters of detail which we need to avoid if we are to keep the present discussion to manageable lengths and not to lose sight altogether of our main concern – the implications of the Internet. Highlighting these two issues – the relation of the individual to the community and the relative priority of the right and the good – may nonetheless serve to cast some light on the theme of this and previous chapters.

In Chapter 5 I set out reasons for thinking that the Internet has the potential for moral anarchy and in Chapter 6 I argued that we can place little hope in countering this tendency by normal conceptions of policing. We may now restate these two claims in the terms which contemporary political philosophy has made familiar, and relate them both to the analysis of community and the contentions of sociologists which occupied us in the first part of this chapter.

Suppose it is indeed the case that in order to deploy a stable and coherent set of values against which to form preferences and make choices, the individual must be radically situated in some form of constituting community. Let us further agree that the mere confluence of interests, subjective and objective, is insufficient for this purpose. The charge against the Internet may then be said to be that, since it permits only the latter (an enclave) and not the former (community properly so-called), it cannot provide an adequate basis for moral life. Moreover, in so far as individuals are drawn more and more to form relationships on the Internet, the world they are entering is indeed one of moral anarchy. Nor is it one that policing in the normal sense could counter, because, for policing to be effective at the deepest level, social regulation must be constructed on the premise that the right takes priority over the good and this, the communitarian alleges, is a doctrine equally flawed.

A doctrine may be false or even incoherent and yet belief in it can have important social consequences. From the fact (if it is one) that the conception of the autonomously deliberating individual, freed from the encumbrances of social norms and communal conventions, is conceptually confused, and that the attempt to secure the priority of the right over the good is no better than chasing a chimera, it does not follow that these are not ideas which cannot be or are not pursued in the non-philosophical worlds of politics and morality. It follows only that they cannot be pursued to any ultimate success. In fact, radical individualism, as a normative doctrine, is alive and well, and one explanation of the findings of the sociologists is that they arise in part precisely from this fruitless pursuit. While it is true (let us suppose) that extraneous social and economic influences have been at work in undermining social networks and institutions, it is also true that the injunction to pursue one's own desires and values, to get what *you* want out of life, is an ideal that has informed a very large part of social education in the Western world this century, emanating, it can be argued, from the hugely influential ideas of the American educationalists John Dewey and G. Stanley Hall. In short, the moral ideal of 'self-realization', even if philosophically incoherent, may nonetheless have been a sort of social acid eating away at the foundation of communities in the proper sense.

Such at any rate is the charge against individualism and against democratic liberalism as its political expression. I do not propose to ask what substance there is to it. It is enough for our purposes that this criticism of liberal individualism is a line of thought with considerable theoretical resources, many prominent adherents and exponents, and that adopting it as a framework for further analysis enables us to return to our central question: is it true that the advent of the Internet is most likely to exacerbate this corrosive ideal, if corrosive it is? Or does the Internet have features which may ameliorate and perhaps even remedy it?

The potential for electronic 'communities'

One way to address this issue is to ask: could the Internet spawn communities in the proper sense? In answering this question an essential step, obviously, is to describe those things among all that goes on there which could provide us with plausible examples. However, in order to do this we need to know what we are looking for and in order to know what we are looking for a little scene-setting is required.

The claim that the Internet is a form of moral anarchy, we may recall, has now been made more precise: the charge is that it intensifies the destructive nature of radical individualism. Assuming it to be true, this implies, as we have seen, that the seeds of individualism are to be found in society more broadly conceived. However theoretically inadequate it may ultimately be, liberal individualism is a highly influential doctrine which has shaped many aspects of life in contemporary Western societies, so much so that it may itself be said to have become a widely held moral ideal. Now if the Internet does free us still further from the encumbrances of the societies to which we belong, it may by this same token enable us to escape the baneful influence of this very ideal. To be enabled thus to transcend the limits of individualism would be to uncover again the possibility of community. The task is to describe in general the means by which this might be done and ask whether we may reasonably expect any of these means to be realized by what we know of the Internet.

Some people do not hesitate to call Internet groups 'communities'. According to Stacy Horn, author of *Cyberville*, an 'electronic salon' such as Echo – the on-line group she established – can be described as a 'virtual community' (the combined term 'virtual salon' is the one she prefers). It is worth speculating on why she says this and what it means. Applying our earlier analysis of the concept of community, we can readily agree that the virtual salon meets the first two criteria. It is a subjective interest group: that is to say, the people who converse within it are interested in the same things. It is also plausible to regard it as an objective interest group: those who use it have material interests in common – the invention of more user-friendly software, the provision of more lines to and from America, for example – though they share these as Internet surfers, not as members of this or that particular group. Even taken together, however, these are not sufficient to make the electric salon a community: it may be an enclave, but it still needs what I have called constituting authority.

As the example of small nomadic communities shows, this does not have to be *an* authority – an identifiable person or office. It is enough if an Internet group like this has admission and exclusion procedures applied by common consensus and special norms of behaviour which determine shared interests in both the objective and the subjective senses. I do not know that this is actually true of Horn's group. But no matter. If and where it is, an Internet group can be said to have the basic elements of a community. Any such group is one to which we belong voluntarily, but not merely in virtue of our interests alone, whether subjective or material. Rather we belong because we accept and adhere to norms and standards (and are required by others to accept and adhere to them) which define and constitute membership, and we remain (because accepted as) members only so long as this is true. To put it in plain though strange-sounding language, there is no reason in principle why an Internet community should not have the same essential features as an order of nuns.

The parallel may seem odd. It is more illuminating than it may at first appear, however – more illuminating, that is to say, with respect to the general issue of individualism. Horn's electric salon is not exclusively a medium of exchange between women, but its electronic character, she claims, has certain important advantages in this respect. The role, place and status of women in contemporary society, even the societies of the West, many feminists have argued, is not that of individuals *per se*. Women are seen not solely, or even primarily, as persons, but as women. This is not a claim I propose to examine or dispute here. It has been made by many writers from a wide variety of disciplines and experience, but its importance for present purposes does not turn upon its truth. Suppose it *is* true. In that event, electronic communication has an advantage for women.

> The only gender differences online are the ones that are ex-pressed with words. You can't see anyone. There's no perfume, no sweat. Nothing soft, nothing hard. We are stripped of ev-erything but our words. And if you take everything away from us but our words, what are the differences between men and women?
>
> (Horn, p. 81)

Those who engage in conversational exchanges in this way, assuming they do not use names that clearly identify them as women, thereby avoid the stock sort of response their thoughts and opinions would elicit if their being female was known to the recipient (whether male or female, we might add). Conversely, they may also find themselves less inhibited. In short, electronic communication could represent a 'gender-blind' form of exchange which is impossible in face-to-face contact. A similar point could be made about race. The Internet is, or can be, colour-blind, and this could equally promote greater freedom of expression and exchange between people of different ethnic origins.

The relative 'blindness' of the Internet is an aspect that can be applied with equal purpose to other groups – the physically handicapped, the elderly and so on. Although it is natural to think of electronic communication as more limited than face-to-face contact, its failure to disclose certain characteristics may in fact make it freer and more fruitful. What these possibilities show is that there is another side to MacIntyre's attack on individualism. 'I am born with a past', he says, 'and to try to cut myself off from that past, in an individualist mode, is to deform my present relationships'. No doubt this is true in many instances, but it is also true that to be able to cut myself off from my past may on occasions allow me to circumvent factors and influences which *also* deform relationships; it all depends on what that past is. African-Americans or women, for example, may be benefited rather than deprived by discarding the legacies bequeathed to them by the communities of which they have been a part.

This point, combined with the suggestion that Internet groups can realize the three conditions required for the existence of a community proper, provides the basis for the idea that the Internet may indeed hold out the possibility of new communities and, depending on how such communities develop in practice, we may find here further support for the suggestion that, far from ushering in an era of total moral anarchy, the Internet promises to supply the means by which the moral anarchy of a world already deleteriously affected by radical individualism may be overcome. There is a countervailing consideration to be brought against this speculation, however, and this is that whatever distorting factors the Internet eliminates, it inevitably introduces even greater ones. What we want to know is not whether communities *of a sort* are possible on the Internet, but whether these can adequately replace (some of) those with which we are more familiar. Is a relationship restricted to electronic communication capable of creating the sort of relationship between human beings that ordinary communities are expected to realize? The answer to this question turns on the *kind* of exchange that is possible by these means.

Stacy Horn speaks of the members of her virtual salon as sharing thoughts and feelings. Now they do so, in the fullest sense, only if thoughts and feelings are wholly communicable by means of words, because it is by means of the written word that Internet relationships are conducted. But it seems evident that this is not so. Our expressive repertoire contains gestures, shrugs, looks and so on. It is by these means no less than by words that we communicate, often very importantly. Moreover, in principle what we 'say' in this way *cannot* be put into words. My hatred, admiration or disgust may be communicated by a look or a gesture and it is genuinely communication. That is to say, by means of such things you get to know, and not to merely guess at, my state of mind and feeling. But it is not a form of communication that admits of linguistic realization. Of course, it is *sometimes* possible to find the words that convey exactly what I am feeling and the more articulate among us are more able to do this fairly readily. But fortunately, inarticulacy is not an absolute bar to communication. If it were, human expression would be much more limited than it is. And it is this inarticulate form (or better, these inarticulate forms) which, as a matter of fact, make up a large part of our communication. Yet the medium of e-mail and similar devices strip us of these no less than it frees us of distorting assumptions. It is not even true that e-mail allows *verbal* exchanges. E-mail, as I noted in an earlier chapter, has gone some way to breaking down traditional differences between the written and the spoken, but one difference between the spoken and the written will always remain: the communicative power of tone of voice and inflection lies in its ability to give the same *words* different *meanings*.

Horn speaks as though disembodied intelligences, by being less restricted or encumbered, are in some sense more pure and hence closer to the 'real' person. Such a contention represents the high-water mark of radical individualism. At work in it, I think, is the old Cartesian idea that persons are essentially minds and their bodies mere appurtenances. It is no accident that Internet groups are sometimes referred to as 'communities of the mind', often with just this implication of a higher, freer form of exchange. But in fact I think the reverse of this sort of Cartesianism is true. Pure *minds* are impoverished *persons*. If this is true then exclusively electronic communication, which consists in linguistic exchanges between disembodied intelligences, is a seriously limited form of communication between persons. It may, it does in fact, make relationships possible and facilitate the confluence of shared interest, but it does so in a restricted form and the restriction means that an Internet community of thought and interest, even if it satisfies the three criteria I set out, is a second-rate form of community.

MUDS, MOOS and *GeoCities*

It might be replied that I have badly slanted the argument against the possibilities of the Internet by identifying electronic communication with linguistic communication and ignoring the visual. It is as though I undertook a discussion of telecommunication and based my conclusions on radio and the telephone to the exclusion of television, when we know full well that in telecommunication the latter is predominant. The difference between e-mail and the Internet, it can be argued, is no less great than the difference between radio and television: in both cases the former is restricted to the linguistic while the latter is not. What difference might this important observation make to talk of new communities?

In discussing this question it is best not to allow much to turn on technical limitations. At present, full audiovisual exchange over the Internet is not possible for any but a very few and there are reasons to think that the World Wide Web, despite its title, will never permit such exchange between all those who might want to use it. Nevertheless, here, as at many previous points in the argument, it needs to be remembered that the Internet is one of the fastest developing technologies the world has ever known and is at an early stage of its development. To rest any claim very heavily on negative speculations about its development is to rely on very weak argumentative grounds. A better approach, therefore, is to allow positive speculation the fullest possible scope and see what can then be said. In any case, the protagonist of the Internet does not need to plunge immediately into the realms of technological speculation at this point. There are *existing* multimedia developments which go some considerable distance beyond e-mail, and provide material for further reflection about communities on the Internet.

Multi-user groups are now no novelty – MUDS (variously 'multi-user directional systems' or 'multi-user dungeons') – and MOOS ('multi-object oriented systems') are familiar in the literature. To belong to a multi-user group means more than electronic correspondence by electronic means: it amounts to conversation among an indefinite number of people uninhibited by time zones and geographical distance, social milieu or political boundaries.

Such conversations can be structured. In Stacy Horn's electronic salon participants divide themselves up by in terms of interest groups – those interested in books or sports and so on. This is relatively simple, but it has the elements of the much more ambitious and complex 'architecture' of *GeoCities*.

GeoCities is the name of one of the first software companies (there are now several others) to supply individual users with very cheap means of creating their own web pages within a structured framework of international proportions. The increase in its popularity is phenomenal. In October 1995 *GeoCities* had 10,000 home pages, by August 1996 100,000 and 1,000,000 in October 1997. By March 1998 it was serving up to 625,000,000 page views per month (a staggering figure when one thinks about it). Given that it is ranked only one of the six principal sites on the Internet, these statistics give some idea of the colossal size and growth of cyberspace as a whole. But it is the distinctive features of *GeoCities* and similar multi-user systems that are of special interest here, and in particular their deployment of 'architecture'. The word 'architecture' used in this context may be a metaphor, but, if it is, it is a very extended one. Those who enter and participate in an electronic GeoCity can find a place for themselves in 'houses' within 'neighbourhoods' within 'cities'. These cities are intended to gather together the like-minded. They have names which indicate the sort of interests and groups that populate them. *Athens*, for example, is peopled by those interested in education, literature and philosophy; *Paris* for romance, poetry and the arts; *Hollywood* for film and TV buffs; *CollegePark* for university academics and students. And so on. Nor is it just subjective interest groups: *Wellesley* is 'a community for women' and *Westhollywood* is a township for 'the gay, lesbian, bisexual and transgendered'.

Within these townships, each user has a 'homesteading site'; there are users who 'live' next door and others who 'live' further off. All these features can be represented visually. Typically the icons supplied reflect something of the spirit of the township. So, for instance, in *Pentagon* the homesteads are military-style tents, while in *Enchanted Forest* (a site for and by children) the homestead icons are 'cute' cottages. Changes can be made to homesteads that are described as 'changing the furniture' or 'moving house', changes which other members of the city can see, appreciate and comment on. It is the possibility of this sort of activity that makes engagement in a GeoCity amount to much more than the passing of messages to and fro.

As the name *M*ulti-*U*ser *D*ungeon*S* suggests, multi-user sites began as games with many players. The vast majority are still devoted, if not to games, at least to the pursuit of leisure activities. This no doubt goes some way to explaining their phenomenal popularity: they combine the attractions of television, computer games and recreational interests with interaction and the ability to tailor what appears on screen. But the existence of sites with much more serious interests – education, gender politics and so on – brings with it the additional possibility that people might pursue something other than leisure by these means. It thus becomes more plausible that these GeoCities should be described as virtual communities. This is not just because the 'architecture' of the GeoCity has a wide range of properties and features that replicate those we find in normal houses and neighbourhoods, and that, like these, structure interaction and exchange. It is also because relationships can be established and explored exclusively in this context. As I noted in an earlier chapter, there are recorded instances of people having met over the Internet and got married, meeting in the flesh for the first time only at the wedding. But there are also recorded instances of people 'marrying' within the 'community' of a GeoCity. That is to say, electronic contact is not the initial step in the relationship, but the whole medium of it. In some GeoCities, political campaigns for 'mayor' and 'sheriff' have been run, and the users elected have had powers of policing and so on, all of an Internet kind of course. In short, both personal and political relationships have been established exclusively within the context of Internet communities. The personal and the political are two important dimensions to human interaction, but we may suppose that other kinds of relationship have been and will increasingly be replicated in this purely electronic medium. (It is familiar now for writers to speak even of 'virtual sex' on the Internet.) It is this, and not their mere multi-user or interactional nature, which raises the question: are these virtual communities new kinds of community in their own right?

The concept of the 'virtual' will provide a major topic for the next chapter, but for the moment we can observe that it is generally taken to signal something which, in some way or other, differs from the normal case. In the case of the GeoCity, this 'something' is not far to seek. The more simple e-mail based discussion groups and the like were found to be lacking in communicative power – a lack which the addition of the visual can go some way to remedy. These GeoCities too lack communicative power – the communicative power that resides in physical touching and feeling. Of course, just as we have reason to think that the move from e-mail to Internet, as from radio to television, constitutes a technological overcoming of this first deficiency, so we might suppose that the technology will be found to overcome the second. Even if we do not know of such things at present, we can speculate that technical means may emerge (are pretty likely to emerge in fact) which would put within our power, electronically speaking, the tangible as well as the visual and the linguistic. This is a line of thought that has no argumentative limit. Whatever deficiency we can identify in the Internet now or in the future, we can equally imagine its being overcome. It follows that Neo-Luddite doubts can never count against any speculation which depends solely on technological innovation. On the other hand, this fact does not give an unqualified advantage to Technophiles. Proponents of the idea that the Internet has the potential for new forms of community face a different difficulty: the more deficiencies the technology of the Internet supplies, the closer it gets to ordinary life, it seems, and the less it can claim real novelty. In short, once all such deficiencies are supplied, Internet communication and exchange will have become communication and exchange as we normally know it.

In fact, in this particular argument between Neo-Luddite and Technophile, the Technophile appears to be caught in a dilemma. Advantages such as those Stacy Horn ascribes to her electronic salon actually *depend* upon its limitations as a form of communication: it is these limits which allow participants to disguise the personal properties – gender, skin colour and so on – which would hinder freedom of exchange. The more those limitations are overcome, the more Internet communities look like ordinary communities, with all their disadvantages – the more, in short, virtual communities come to look like the normal thing.

This is a line of thought which we will have to take up again. However, there is at least one further rejoinder that the Technophile can make at this point and which places the discussion in a rather wider context. The phrase 'virtual reality' is normally taken to imply 'as good as the real thing'; perhaps, properly understood, it is *better* than the real thing, at least for certain purposes. Whether this appeal to virtual reality makes a difference or not is, as we shall see, a question whose principal importance lies in its connection with the topic of community. But initially, at any rate, it has dimensions sufficiently independent to warrant a new chapter – the next, and final, one.

8 Virtual reality

The future of cyberspace

With the concept of 'virtual reality' we arrive at the world of science fiction and of fantasy. Or so many suppose, and it may indeed seem that if in the discussion of virtual reality every limit on the imagination is removed, then all the factual and conceptual constraints which control our speculations are lifted also. Such a lack of constraint may suit the novelist or storyteller, but it is a freedom we do not want in the sort of inquiry we are engaged in here, because it makes any speculation as good as every other and hence marks the end of serious critical investigation. Actually, although in discussing virtual reality we are indeed entering the realms of the highly speculative, the position should not be construed as one quite without constraint. What is true is that we need to be careful about the constraints we observe. As I remarked at the start of the book, and have had occasion to repeat in the ensuing argument, the sheer speed at which the technology of the Internet is developing is probably unprecedented in human history, and for this reason there is a constant danger of declaring something to be impossible a priori, only to find that in a very short time it is a reality. The same thing can be said of VR technology, which has largely been developed independently of the Internet.

The 'bodynet' and the 'smartroom'

Nevertheless, though the future undoubtedly holds many hitherto undreamt of technical marvels, what is *imaginable* is not necessarily *conceivable*. The distinction is illustrated with great regularity in traditional fairy stories. We can imagine, easily enough, that the prince is turned into a frog, but there are well-known philosophical obstacles in the way of making such an imaginary event properly intelligible. The same sort of thing is observable in science fiction. There are many tales of time travellers, and very entertaining and diverting they can be. But philosophers know well that whether time travel is conceptually possible is a vexed and difficult question. A large part of its difficulty lies in the fact that the idea of time travel seems to admit the flatly contradictory – the traveller existing before he was born, for instance, or encountering on his travels a younger person who both is and is not himself. Contradictory states of affairs are as good a mark of the impossible as one can hope to find, but even so we can *imagine* the contradictory without any great difficulty, as when we picture (either mentally or with pen and ink) the older and the younger time traveller meeting each other.

From this it follows that not all that is imaginable is conceivable. We can imagine things which logically could not happen, and if they are indeed logically impossible, necessarily they are empirically impossible also. To make any headway with the idea of virtual reality and hence with the future of cyberspace, then, we need to restrict ourselves to the realms of the conceptually possible and ignore the impossible imaginings of science-fiction writers. At the same time, if we are to think about the future of cyberspace to any real purpose, then, to reiterate what was said in the previous chapter, we should allow full rein to speculation about the *technically* possible. At present, life on the Internet does not amount to much more than interactive television. People have speculated, however, that whenever the devices of VR technology that might be developed in the future can be plugged into the Internet, the result will be something much more like a 'total' experience. One of the steps along the way to this is the 'bodynet', described by one of the most enthusiastic futurists in the world of information technology as follows:

> The bodynet is the brainchild of Olin Shivers at the MIT Laboratory for Computer Science ... The Shivers bodynet

builds on a pair of 'magic glasses' that you wear. They have clear lenses that let you see where you are going but also present miniature inset displays that show color images to each eye. The images are generated by a computer the size of a cigarette pack on your belt or in your purse. The glasses also have photodiode sensors that monitor the whites of your eyes in order to detect where you're looking. Miniature microphones and earphones attached to the glasses let you speak to and hear from your equipment ... The gadgets communicate with one another in a language called 'bodytalk', which is transmitted via low-power radio waves that are confined to an invisible envelope around your body – the body network, or bodynet.

(Dertouzos, p. 64–5)

The bodynet, or the 'smartroom' (another very hi-tech device described by Dertouzos), is not necessarily linked to the pursuit of virtual reality, but clearly has or is expected to have implications in this connection. For convenience devices such as these and speculations about their possible uses can be combined into what is sometimes known as a 'VR Body Zone'. The aspiration behind the VR Body Zone is that it would make Internet encounters far less like watching television and more like experiencing the real thing. And it is to the world of the Internet *with* such a device, rather than that now currently prevailing, that the term 'virtual reality' is normally applied.

Let us grant the Internet enthusiasts and futurists all the advances and advantages that these technological speculations permit and let us for the moment deploy the phrase 'virtual reality' to indicate the kind of experience that electronic communication up to and including such devices would make possible. We can then ask the following questions. Is virtual reality in any sense a new mode of being, and in so far as it is, is it better or worse than the everyday world with which we are all familiar?

The 'virtual' and the 'real thing'

Consider other examples of the use of 'virtual'. In the expression 'virtual certainty' the word 'virtual' implies 'as good as'. When something is a virtual certainty, then, even though it is *not* certain, it can be taken to be so, at any rate for the purposes in hand. In so far as it has any currency, the expression 'virtual reality' seems to function in a similar way. It signals something not the same as, but as good as, the real thing, at least for certain purposes. Of course, in making sense of this a lot turns on what we mean by the 'real thing', but I do not think we need to spell this out in the abstract. In any individual case it will be clear enough. To have met a virtually real Marilyn Monroe is as good as having met her in the flesh; to have climbed the Eiger in virtual reality is as good as having climbed the Eiger; to have 'virtually' encountered a man-eating tiger in the depths of the South East Asian jungle is as good as having encountered a real one. To each of these examples we must add, of course, the qualification 'for certain purposes'. What might those purposes be? The last example gives us a clue. For the purposes of knowing 'what it is like' to meet a man-eating tiger, a virtual one is as good as a real one and it has the further advantage of none of the normal risks attaching. One can extend the example certainly and imagine being 'virtually eaten' by the virtual tiger, and hence getting to know what it is like to be eaten by a tiger. Still, no death results and this has to be an advantage virtual reality enjoys over the real thing.

The extension of the man-eating tiger example might be thought to bring us not so much to the realms of the fantastic as the ludicrous. And so perhaps it does. But it allows us to raise two important doubts about virtual reality. First, do we really find out 'what it is like' to face a man-eating tiger if we know that there is no danger of actually being eaten? Second, do we need all the apparatus of the bodynet and the smartroom to accomplish this? It will be most convenient to begin with the second of these questions.

Are people in the networked VR Body Zone so very different from the person stimulated by and caught up in far simpler forms of make-believe? At a minimum, it is not obvious that they are, because the ordinary power of make-believe is very considerable. This is a fact about the arts in general that has been taken up by Kendall Walton, author of a major study in aesthetics entitled *Mimesis as Make-believe*. An important part of his thesis is that the world of make-believe as embodied in films, plays, novels and other forms of artistic imagination allows us to 'enjoy' the experiences depicted without the normal costs of doing so.

> Make-believe … is a truly remarkable invention. We can … make sure the good guys win, or see what it is like for the bad guys to win … There is a price to pay in real life when the bad guys win, even if we learn from experience. Make-believe provides the experience – something like it anyway – for free. The divergence between fictionality and truth spares us pain and suffering we would have to experience in the real world. We realize some of the benefits of hard experience without having to undergo it.
>
> (Walton, p. 68)

Whether this is a good explanation of the value of works of art is open to question, but that is not the issue here. Rather, we want to know whether the vaunted advantages of an Internet capable of full-blooded virtual reality effects constitutes something radically new. And the answer seems to be that it is not: certainly it may be true that virtual reality 'provides the experience – something like it anyway – for free', but this is no more than Walton claims for the 'remarkable invention' of make-believe as exhibited in less technically advanced media such as plays, novels and films.

To see that there really is no very great difference here despite the futuristic nature of cyberspace, something more needs to be said about the relation between, on the one hand, having the experience 'what it is like to … ' and, on the other, any given medium that induces this. Suppose that I am reading a narrative of encountering a tiger in a jungle. It might be fiction, or it might be the reporting of fact, but in the hands of a good author either might induce in me a sense of 'knowing what it is like'. Of course there is certainly a difference between knowing what it is like in virtue of reading an account and knowing what it is like because I have

myself been in this circumstance. An important part of the difference lies in this simple fact: in the first case, though I 'know what
it is like', it is not true of me that I have encountered a tiger; in the
second case, it *is* true that I have encountered the real thing, and it
is precisely because this is true that I know what it is like. However,
this difference applies just as well to my encounter with a virtual
tiger as to my merely reading about it. In this case too, however
life-like the virtual experience of a tiger, it is not *actually* an experience of a tiger and no increase in technical sophistication will
make it so.

There are prospective differences between storytelling and VR
experiences, certainly, just as there are differences between a film
and a novel. But since in both cases the impression, however vivid,
necessarily falls short of the reality, any such differences, whether
between storytelling and virtual reality or between film and literature, must lie in the nature of the alternative media. 'Knowing
what it is like' is the same in both cases; all that differs is the
means by which this has been induced.

It seems plausible to characterize this difference in the following
way. The story-book case relies upon my imagination, aided no
doubt by the imaginative and descriptive power of the author. The
virtual reality case, by contrast, leaves much less to my imagination, perhaps hardly anything at all, because the gap between experience and reality which imagination normally bridges is filled
by the technical devices of the electronic medium.

It is tempting to try to strengthen this point by saying: reading
about tigers is *not at all like* encountering tigers, whereas virtual
experience of a tiger is *very like* actual experience of a tiger. Let us
agree that this is true. Nevertheless, if the point or value of the virtual experience is coming to know 'what it is like', this is also the
case in the imaginative experience prompted by my reading. What
is called virtual reality may have the advantage of inducing this
sense of 'what it is like' more easily, and perhaps more vividly, especially among the less imaginative, but it still remains the case
that if the merit of virtual reality is said to lie in its being 'as good
as' the real thing for the purpose of coming to know 'what it is
like', this is true of other much less technically complex media
also.

Despite the difficulty of discerning any very great distinction between media such as novels and films with which we are thoroughly familiar and Virtual Body Zones yet to be invented, the idea is likely to persist, I think, that a virtual reality experience of X is in some important and interesting way *closer* to the actual experience of X than is merely reading or seeing a film about X. But on what might this greater closeness be based? One common answer is that virtual reality experiences are (or would be at any rate) 'just like' the real thing. Is this true? Here there is reason to return to the first of the two questions posed earlier. Do we really find out 'what it is like' to face a man-eating tiger if we know that there is no danger of actually being eaten? Suppose we answer 'No' to this question with respect to novels and plays. Then we must also answer 'No' in the case of virtual reality. This is because however vivid the experience inside our wraparound goggles and data gloves, we know we are not in danger of being eaten just as much as we know it when we sit and read the book. Many people, I imagine, would feel inclined to answer 'Yes' with respect to virtual reality machines, to say that in the case of virtual reality we really *do* get to know what it is like to face a man-eating tiger even though we know there is no chance of our being eaten. The temptation to say this is because we can predict that under such circumstances people are likely to experience the same emotions and exhibit the same reactions that they would in the presence of an actual tiger – terror, anxiety and so on. But on exactly the same grounds we would have to answer 'Yes' in the case of other media also because it is a fact (much discussed by philosophers of art) that novels, films and plays can stir strong emotional reactions on the part of audiences – horror at horror films, sadness at tragedies and so on – even in the familiar surroundings of their own homes. It follows, it seems to me, that either way we have no reason to attribute any difference *in kind* to virtual reality experiences over other make-believe experiences. At most, we have reason to attribute a difference of degree of vividness or intensity.

The reason for this is that on the analysis so far, even the most technically sophisticated virtual reality set-ups must be interpreted as experiences without 'the reality'. What is missing, it appears, is any ingredient that would incline us to say that virtual reality is more than a simulacrum – that it is a different *kind* of reality, different but just as good as (or better than) any other for certain purposes.

'Virtual' as a kind of reality

The previous chapter was concerned with Internet communities. These, as we noted, are frequently referred to as 'virtual communities' and it was this expression which led us on to the discussion of virtual reality, the 'reality' of which we have now found reason to doubt. It seems, though, that the use of 'virtual' in 'virtual community' signals something a little different from its use in the more general expression 'virtual reality'. A virtual community is not a community that is an experientially indistinguishable copy of the real thing, but rather a community of a different kind. In this sense 'virtual' signals not a simulacrum of reality, but a different kind of reality, and this is just the idea we want to explore.

It was Howard Rheingold, author of *The Virtual Community: Homesteading on the Electronic Frontier*, who first brought this use of the term to prominence and who provides a definition that has gained a certain currency:

> virtual communities are social aggregations that emerge from the Net when enough people carry on ... public discussions long enough, with sufficient human feeling, to form webs of personal relationships in cyberspace.
>
> (Rheingold, p. 5)

The first thing to be observed about this definition is that it contains no reference to (or even hint of) substitute experience. Nothing said here suggests that the emergence of a virtual community depends on or would even be specially advanced by the development of hi-tech Virtual Body Zones. The contrast, it appears, is not between that of a 'real' community of flesh-and-blood people and an experiential simulacrum which conveys what the real thing is like. The difference lies elsewhere. Where could this be? The answer will be found, I think, by remembering the origins of the virtual community. MUDS and MOOS, out of which those groups called virtual communities have emerged, were first devised as many-player games. So the question is: when does interacting on the Internet in a structured way cease to be merely a game? When does it take on the seriousness (rather than the feel) of community life? The answer in outline is: when a *virtual* community is formed, and this is precisely the point which Rheingold's definition aims to capture or isolate (whether or not it succeeds).

In this sense of 'virtual', the virtual is not a semblance of something else, but an alternative to it – an alternative type of entity with properties both similar and dissimilar to that with which it is contrasted. If this is correct, the question is whether this alternative form of community is a kind of entity in its own right, and of a sort that allows us to attribute to it a distinctive form of reality.

Why should anyone deny this, or deny that virtual communities, though different are real enough in their own way? The crucial difference between 'encountering a tiger' or 'climbing the Eiger' by means of a VR Body Zone and doing these things in real life can, as we saw, be expressed in terms of make-believe. It is possible (in theory) by means of VR to have the experience of encountering a tiger (or something like it) but this is really no different to having 'made-believe' with the help of a novel or a film that I have met a tiger. In the absence of the real thing it remains true of me that I have never *as a matter of fact* encountered a tiger. Imagine, now, someone whose sole experience of interacting with others lay, or at least had come to lie, in relationships formed within a GeoCity or virtual community. Would it be true of such a person that they had never 'really' interacted with anyone, that they merely knew 'what it was like' to do so? The answer is much less obvious than in the VR case and this is why there is some reason to attribute to virtual communities a reality of their own.

Why is the answer only *much less* clear? Why is it not plain that they have indeed formed real relationships, though of a different sort? The residual doubt arises from this important fact: it seems possible that indefinitely many of the relationships they enter into by this means are fictional. At this point we return, in fact, to the discussion suspended at the end of the previous chapter.

A virtual community could in theory comprise the one real person we are hypothesizing (for convenience, our real person can be a woman called Technos) and indefinitely many invented personalities. If Technos does not know this, and believes that she has friends and acquaintances with whom she exchanges gossip, from whom she learns and to whom she turns for advice, is she not deluded? There *are* no friends out there, only invented personalities, so how can she have real relationships with them? Alter the case so that Technos has herself invented the larger part of the character by which she represents herself on the Internet. The whole thing now seems a delusion, no better than a game and possibly worse in so far as it has generated a degree of deception.

But is the resultant community life truly a delusion? The case in which all the characters in a virtual community are significantly different to the real-life 'players' who 'operate' them, is certainly the most interesting case to explore. If under these circumstances we could find a way of attributing a certain sort of reality to the community they comprise, we should indeed have found a virtual reality of an interestingly different kind. The principal difficulty in the way of spelling this possibility out convincingly lies, of course, in the thought that such a community would in fact have returned to that from which it had its origin – namely a mere game. What we need to ask, therefore, is whether the wholly fictional community just imagined could have the sort of seriousness that Rheingold builds into his definition, or whether it would be nothing more than a game of very great sophistication.

'Virtual' achievements

To simplify the task of exploring this question I shall introduce some stipulative terminology. Let us use the term 'community' to refer to the normal case – the villages, associations, cities and countries with which we are familiar, whether or not these meet the stricter criteria of a 'community' that we set out in the previous chapter. And, ignoring the fact that many of the Internet groups currently referred to as virtual communities are 'inhabited' by real people, let us reserve the term 'virtual community' for an Internet group in which all the on-screen personalities are the *alter egos* of those who, so to speak, sit at their terminals. Is a virtual community in this limited sense anything more than a game?

Computer games have something in common with VR. In a computer game I 'kill', let us say, a number of evil invaders. Of course, in an obvious sense, it is true that even so I have never actually killed anyone. That is to say, just as in the earlier example where my 'VR encountering' a tiger falls short of actually encountering a tiger, however life-like the experience, in the game there is a similar falling short with respect to 'killing' invaders. Nevertheless, there is a difference and one which, we might say, makes all the difference, for killing enough invaders in the game counts not as an imaginary win, but a *real* one. In other words 'killing game invaders', though different from 'killing real invaders', is still an achievement. It is not the *same* achievement, but an achievement nonetheless – an achievement within the game. Similarly, a relationship established by Technos, though not a relationship with the person at the other terminal, is a relationship 'within the virtual community'. Two questions arise. First, does this remain true if Technos is herself an invented persona? Second, if it does, is this enough to make the relationship thereby achieved something other than a move in a game?

We can expand the example in ways which allow us to explore these questions further. Imagine that Technos gets elected mayor of the virtual community (let us call it Cyberville) and initiates a building programme. A 'law' is established by which every time someone comes on-line, their persona has to contribute to the emerging communal construction by the addition of a suitable building icon. Failure to do so results in exclusion. Over time, this cooperative activity results in Cyberville's having the most sophisticated architectural construction of any virtual community to be found on the Internet. Then Technos starts to make 'political' misjudgements and the policies she pursues lead to dissension. So great is this dissension that more and more personae leave Cyberville until, finally, it is abandoned and the virtual community known as Cyberville ceases to exist. It becomes, in other words, a 'ghost town on the electronic frontier' just like so many on the original Frontier. Could we not say that the architectural construction which lasted for a time was a significant achievement and that Technos's mismanagement of the virtual community was, correspondingly, a significant failure? If we can say this then, as it seems to me, we have given sense to the idea that Cyberville is (or was) a community in a different order of reality and thus something more substantial than a mere game.

To decide whether this is the right conclusion to draw, we have to describe the history of Cyberville with some care. Despite the way I have just posed the question, the crucial point is not so much whether an achievement or a failure 'within the virtual community' is a move in a game, but whether either the achievement or the failure can properly be attributed to the personae who inhabit this community. Did the inhabitants build an impressive structure? Did Technos fail the community as mayor? It seems there is reason to doubt this, because it seems odd to say that the public policy which proved disastrous was decided by Technos. Isn't it more plausible to hold that the policy was decided by the *author* of Technos – the person who sat at the terminal? Suppose that Technos has an arrogant and autocratic temperament, while the author of Technos is not like this at all, and that it is because of this arrogance and autocracy that the policy failed. Even so, we have not eliminated the ultimate responsibility of the author, because it is the author who has decided that Technos shall have this character, and who, step by step, has authored the reactions and responses which best express this temperament. In short, it appears that at some point or other we must make reference to real persons and cannot explain the whole history of Cyberville entirely in terms of the invented personae who constitute the virtual community.

This does not show, however, that it is all a game. For a time the author of Technos has successfully presided over a functioning community which has to its credit an electronic construction of impressive proportions. The truth of this is not altered by the fact that the people of Cyberville are fictions or that the basis of the construction is digital information held on servers rather than bricks and mortar existing in physical space. Asked the question: 'What have you ever achieved?' the author of Technos can truthfully point to a community and an architectural construction which really existed – *really* existed in cyberspace. This reveals a difference with the earlier virtual reality examples. There the person who, thanks to the VR Body Zone, had the experience of encountering a tiger can say 'I know what it is like to encounter a tiger' but cannot say 'I have encountered a tiger'. By contrast, the author of Technos can say *both* 'I know what it is like to preside over a community' *and* 'I have presided over a community'. Moreover, she can say the former precisely because she can truly say the latter.

I have chosen this particular example with care because it is not clear that the same point could be made about all relationships established within a virtual community. Imagine another invented persona: Webman. Let us suppose that, on some level of description or other, Webman and Technos fall in love, marry and set up a new home in Cyberville. On the strength of this it seems plausible to think that the author of Technos could claim that she knew what it was like to be in love, but not that she had been in love. From this is follows that only *some* Internet relationships and activities can count as real achievements as opposed to simulated achievements like those we experience in the VR Body Zone, and in turn this implies that the distinctive reality which is to be found in virtual communities may be importantly limited.

Still, the general point is this. Virtual reality – interpreted not as simulation but as the sort of world realized in the virtual community just described – can properly be conceived of as a distinctive mode of existence, a mode that is not just a game, but a world of its own in which a significant if limited range of things can be accomplished and lost. If we now add to this minimal claim the reminder that the Internet is at a very early stage of development, there is reason to think the future of cyberspace will bring metaphysical novelties – that virtual reality interpreted via the virtual community is to some extent a new world and one that we are on the edge of.

To make this notion of a metaphysical novelty clearer it may be useful to consider what has been called the 'cyberstore' – an Internet site where a wide variety of goods can be inspected and ordered. According to Neil Barrett, the cyberstore

> can be represented as a virtual reality implementation of the largest, flagship megastore. Consumers can ... move through the cyberstore using a mouse or keyboard to direct their

search. Shelves full of goods can be displayed and the shopper can select and sample goods – perhaps simply by 'clicking' on the image.

(Barrett, p. 112)

Internet shopping is now fairly commonplace and growing rapidly. The Internet bookstore Amazon.com has reported annual increases in sales of over 480 per cent. Much of it, however, is simply a matter of doing by other means what we have done for centuries. We order a book, say, but the book is dispatched from an ordinary warehouse by ordinary means. More interesting are the cyberstores which sell only electronic goods – texts, films, music – that are downloaded direct to the purchaser's PC and paid for by a credit-card system that is wholly electronic, with earnings attributed to the earner through BCTS (the computerised Bank Credit Transfer System). Such a cyberstore operates wholly within the world of the Internet and the point at which it 'touches' the ordinary world is only at the point of consumption and consumer satisfaction. What it sells, however, is substantial enough. Though neither the goods, nor their transfer, nor the financial transaction has any ordinary physical embodiment, these are *real* goods and sales and transfers – virtually real perhaps but real nonetheless. The point is, they are of a kind that could not have existed before the advent of the Internet and the World Wide Web.

The poverty of cyberspace

Virtual reality interpreted in this way, then, is a kind of reality and not merely a copy or simulation of something else. There remains this all-important issue. Even if there is indeed a new world coming into view, not just in a metaphorical but in a metaphysical sense, have we any special reason to welcome it? The answer to this question turns, as it seems to me, on what we can say about the value of this new medium relative to other media that it might replace. Once more, in order to simplify the discussion, I shall make a stipulation and from here on use the expression 'virtual reality' to mean the medium which the examples of Technos, Cyberville and the virtual megastore have isolated, ignoring any special connection it normally has with VR Body Zones and the like.

Why would we favour community life in virtual reality rather than community life on the streets, so to speak? One possible explanation lies with the account Walton gives of make-believe. His claim, it will be recalled, is that 'there is a price to pay in real life when the bad guys win, even if we learn from experience. Make-believe provides the experience ... for free'. It is not hard to see how this line of thought applies to Cyberville. 'For free' is not quite right, however. While there is clearly a price to pay when real communities break up in dissension and strife, there is also a price to pay for the break-up of a virtual community. But it is not the same and certainly not as high. No actual bones are broken, no blood spilt, no buildings or businesses destroyed. What is destroyed is the virtual community itself and the virtually real accomplishments which have resulted from its existence. If we take Rheingold's definition seriously, the building of communities in virtual reality includes 'sufficient human feeling' and this feeling will be dissipated and frustrated. It is not itself 'virtual' feeling, but the emotion invested by the authors of Technos, Webman and all the other personae. This is a real cost. Still, it is a cost that falls short of the losses sustained by those whose ordinary homes and communities are the casualties of civil strife.

One thought which this prompts is that, given a choice, human beings would risk less by engaging in virtual relationships than in ordinary ones. Might this be the attraction of the world of virtual reality? The answer depends on a trade-off between the diminished risk and the more limited character of such engagements. In advance of knowing the future character of cyberspace, this is a calculation that is hard to make. Nevertheless, there seems reason to suppose that the limitations of cyberspace will always be greater than those which operate on corresponding relations in ordinary life and consequently that the reduced risks will not outweigh the loss of possible benefits. Anyone who has followed the exploration of this chapter, in fact, could hardly conclude anything but that virtual communities are relatively poor substitutes for real ones. Their poverty does not lie in their being mere simulacra, as is the case for VR Body Zone experiences, which as we saw lack the crucial element of reality. But on present reckoning, and as far into the future as one can reasonably see, they are impoverished nonetheless. The possibilities of virtual reality may well bring added benefits, but without the context of ordinary life, to live one's life primarily on the Internet would be a poor way to be.

In this chapter we have been exploring the outer reaches of the Internet. Previous chapters were concerned with its more mundane implications. It is time now to try to summarize our findings in a conclusion.

Conclusion

In the early 1890s a US newspaper syndicate surveyed seventy-four eminent American men and women about life in 1993, and it published the results for the Chicago World's Columbian Exposition of 1893. Dave Walter has compiled their responses in a fascinating book, and they show the perils of technological extrapolation. What is remarkable is not any omission of nuclear weapons or microelectronics; many public figures of the late nineteenth century foresaw both new weapons of mass destruction and new forms of electrically powered global communication. The striking oversight is the rise of mass motoring. Nobody understood the chain of technological, commercial, social and political events that would surround the internal combustion engine which Karl Benz had patented in 1886.

(Tenner, p. x)

Given the huge effect that the private motor car has had on almost every aspect of human life, this was an oversight of monumental proportions. Yet there does not seem any reason why the people canvassed *should* have foreseen it. With the Internet the position is a little different. We are already some way down the road of its development, and we know something of the scale and speed at which it is developing. Nevertheless, whether the road in question will actually be the information superhighway that futurists and enthusiasts predict is still uncertain. What we do know is that all such prediction is fraught with difficulty. Does it not follow that any investigation of the implications of the Internet is bound to fail?

This is a question I raised at the outset of this book and claimed that only the course of argument itself could answer it. Has it been answered and, if so, how? It is not difficult to state some of the conclusions succinctly: the truth about the Internet lies somewhere between the fears of the Neo-Luddites and the hopes of the Technophiles; technological innovation cannot and should not be regarded merely as an improved means to a pre-selected end because while some technology merely modifies, other technology transforms, and with respect to a number of areas of existence we may expect the Internet to be transforming. It will not, however, transform political life along more truly democratic lines, or, rather, in so far as it does it will strengthen the downside of democracy which has a tendency to favour consumer politics over rational decision-making. In all probability it will strengthen rather than weaken the atomizing character of individualism because it encourages moral fragmentation, and neither externalist attempts to police it nor the internal formation of virtual communities is likely to counter such a tendency effectively. At the same time, it does not have a very great deal to offer by way of a compensating virtual reality, if we remember the similar advantages that we can derive from much older forms of make-believe.

Thus succinctly stated, the conclusions sound much more negative than positive. To a degree this is true, but they are negative largely in relation to the somewhat wide-eyed hopes of the Technophiles. It is certainly the case, in my view, that the Internet has brought and will continue to bring new benefits, interests and possibilities on a scale so large that in a relatively short time to be linked to it will be as beneficial, and as troublesome, but nonetheless as necessary as having a telephone or a motor car. And like these things it will alter our mode of existence – but the degree to which the motor car and the telephone have done this, though very great, can be exaggerated too. 'In this world', Benjamin Franklin famously said, 'nothing is certain but death and taxes.' But surely other things can be said to be certain also: those aspects of existence which can be described as features of human nature and the human condition. People will continue to have and to value emotional and creative lives broadly similar to those they have always had. If the changes wrought by the motor car and the telephone are striking, it is no less striking that, for all the vast differences between their worlds and ours, people continue to read, study and value Plato, the Psalmists, Augustine, Shakespeare, Omar Khayyam, Newton, Donne, Tolstoy and countless others. Conversely, they will continue to share many of the difficulties that beset every age. Modern technology may have made huge advances in helping us cope with illness and poverty (though these can be exaggerated) but it is as foolish to believe that technology will *abolish* disease or destitution as it is to believe that cryonics could be an effective way of overcoming death. There is no sign that the sources, as opposed to the means, of war, or the difficulty of securing peace, are much altered by technological advance, and the ever-present possibility of suicide, of which existentialist philosophers made so much, is not the sort of thing that could be removed by digital information technology, however cheap and powerful.

If this is true, we may expect the Internet to be tempered by human nature and the human condition as much as, indeed more than, we may expect it to transform them, and this tells us something about Faustian bargains. As we saw, the transforming and unpredictable character of technological innovation makes any manageable form of cost–benefit analysis impossible. Does this mean that we have no way by which to judge it? No, because all such technology comes into existence and develops in a context, and that context at its broadest is the one to which reference has just been made – human nature and the human condition. It is a context, however, which bears on our assessment of technology not by providing a medium in which costs and benefits may be compared, but by providing us with the standard against which the ultimate value of technology must be measured. As Heidegger saw, from a rather different philosophical perspective than that from which I have been working, ultimately 'The Question Concerning Technology' is directly related to what it means to *be*.

Bibliography

Bacon, F., *The New Organon*, Indianapolis, Bobbs-Merrill Educational Publishing, 1960.

Barrett, N., *The State of the Cybernation*, London, Kogan Page, 1996.

Bellah, R., Madsen, R., Sullivan, W.M., Swidler, A. and Tipton, S.M., *Habits of the Heart: Individualism and Commitment in American Life*, Berkeley, University of California Press, 1985.

Benedikt, M. (ed.), *Cyberspace: First Steps*, Cambridge, MA, MIT Press, 1991.

Berry, W., 'Why I Am Not Going to Buy a Computer', *What Are People For?*, San Francisco, North Point Press, 1990.

Boal, I.A. and Brook, J. (eds), *Resisting the Virtual Life: The Culture and Politics of Information*, San Francisco, City Lights, 1995.

Boorstin, D.J., *The Americans: The Colonial Experience*, New York, Vintage Books, 1958.

—— *The Americans: The Democratic Experience*, New York, Vintage Books, 1974.

—— *The Americans: The National Experience*, New York, Sphere Books, 1988.

Borgmann, A., *Technology and the Character of Contemporary Life: A Philosophical Inquiry*, Chicago, University of Chicago Press, 1984.

Burke, E., *On Government, Politics and Society*, Glasgow, Fontana/The Harvester Press, 1975.

Cohen, G.A., *Karl Marx's Theory of History: A Defence*, Oxford, Clarendon Press, 1978.

Conley, V.A. (ed.) on behalf of the Miami Theory Collective, *Rethinking Technologies*, Minneapolis, University of Minnesota Press, 1993.

Dertouzos, M.L., *What Will Be: How the New World of Information Will Change Our Lives*, London, Piatkus, 1997.

Devlin, P., *The Enforcement of Morals*, Oxford, Oxford University Press, 1965.

Dyson, F., *Imagined Worlds*, Cambridge, MA, Harvard University Press, 1997.

Easton, S.M., *The Problem of Pornography: Regulation and the Right to Free Speech*, London, Routledge, 1994.

Elton, M., 'I Can't Believe It's Not Real: Reflections on Virtual Reality', *Ends and Means* 3 (1998), pp. 21–8.

Evans-Pritchard, E.E., *Witchcraft, Oracles and Magic Among the Azande*, Oxford, Clarendon Press, 1937.

Gates, B., *The Road Ahead*, New York, Viking Penguin, 1995.

Graham, G., *Contemporary Social Philosophy*, Oxford, Basil Blackwell, 1990.

—— 'Liberalism and Democracy', *Journal of Applied Philosophy* 9 (1992), pp. 149–60.

—— 'Anarchy of the Internet', *Ends and Means* 1 (1996), pp. 24–7.

—— *The Shape of the Past: A Philosophical Approach to History*, Oxford, Oxford University Press, 1997.

Graham, K., *The Battle of Democracy: Conflict, Consensus and the Individual*, Brighton, Wheatsheaf Books, 1986.

Gray, T., *Freedom*, Atlantic Cliffs, Humanities Press International, 1991.

Harasim, L.M. (ed.), *Global Networks: Computers and International Communication*, Thousand Oaks, Sage Publications, 1995.

Harrison, R., *Democracy*, London, Routledge, 1993.

Heidegger, M., 'The Question Concerning Technology', in D.F. Krell (ed.), *Basic Writings*, London, Routledge, 1993.

Heim, M., *Virtual Realism*, Oxford, Oxford University Press, 1998.

Heyd, D. (ed.), *Toleration: An Elusive Virtue*, Princeton, Princeton University Press, 1996.

Hobbes, T., *Leviathan: or the Matter, Forme and Power of a Commonwealth Ecclesiasticall and Civil*, Oxford, Basil Blackwell, 1960.

Horn, S., *Cyberville*, New York, Warner Books, 1998.

Hume, D., *A Treatise of Human Nature*, Oxford, Clarendon Press, 1967.

Johnson, S., *Interface Culture: How New Technology Transforms the Way We Create and Communicate*, San Francisco, HarperEdge, 1997.

Jones, S.G. (ed.), *CyberSociety: Computer-Mediated Communication and Community*, Thousand Oaks, Sage Publications, 1995.

Kant, I., *Critique of Pure Reason*, trans. N.K. Smith, London, MacMillan, 1929.

—— *Foundations of the Metaphysics of Morals*, trans. L.W. Beck, Indianapolis, Bobbs-Merrill Educational Publishing, 1959.

Kieran, M. (ed.), *Media Ethics*, London, Routledge, 1998.

Kujundzic, N. and Mann, D., 'The Unabomber, the Economics of Happiness, and the End of the Millennium', *Ends and Means* 3 (1998), pp. 11–20.

Leyton, E., *Hunting Humans*, Tundra Books/McClelland & Stewart, 1995.

Locke, J., *Two Treatises of Government*, New York, Cambridge University Press, 1960.

MacIntyre, A., *After Virtue: A Study in Moral Theory*, London, Duckworth, 1981.

Marx, K. and Engels, F., *The Communist Manifesto*, Harmondsworth, Penguin, 1968.

—— *The German Ideology*, New York, International Publishers, 1968.

Matthews, E., 'Medical Technology and the Concept of Healthcare', *Ends and Means* 1 (1996), pp. 18–20.

Mill, J.S., *On Liberty and Other Writings*, Cambridge, Cambridge University Press, 1989.

Woonteiler, D. (ed.) on behalf of O'Reilly and Associates Inc., *The Harvard Conference on the Internet and Society*, Cambridge, MA, Harvard University Press, 1997.

Petroshi, H., *Engineers of Dreams*, New York, Vintage Books, 1995.

Porter, R., *The Greatest Benefit to Mankind: A Medical History of Humanity from Antiquity to the Present*, London, HarperCollins, 1997.

Postman, N., *Amusing Ourselves to Death*, London, Methuen, 1987.

—— *Technopoly: The Surrender of Culture to Technology*, New York, Vintage Books, 1993.

Puttnam, R.D., 'Tuning In, Tuning Out: The Strange Disappearance of Social Capital in America', *Political Science* 47 (1995), pp. 664–5.

Rawls, J., *A Theory of Justice*, Oxford, Oxford University Press, 1972.

Rheingold, H., *The Virtual Community: Homesteading on the Electronic Frontier*, Reading, MA, Addison-Wesley Publishing Co., 1993.

Rousseau, J.-J., *The Social Contract*, Oxford, Oxford University Press, 1994.

Sandel, M.J., *Liberalism and the Limits of Justice*, Cambridge, Cambridge University Press, 1982.

Schuler, D., *New Community Networks: Wired for Change*, New York, ACM Press, 1996.

Shields, R. (ed.), *Cultures of Internet: Virtual Spaces, Real Histories, Living Bodies*, London, Sage Publications, 1996.

Stocks, J.L., *Morality and Purpose*, ed. D.Z. Phillips, London, Routledge & Kegan Paul, 1969.

Stoll, C., *Silicon Snake Oil: Second Thoughts on the Information Highway*, New York, Doubleday, 1995.

Taylor, M., *Community, Anarchy and Liberty*, Cambridge, Cambridge University Press, 1982.

Tenner, E., *Why Things Bite Back: Technology and the Revenge Effect*, London, Fourth Estate, 1996.

Toulmin, S., *Foresight and Understanding*, London, Hutchinson, 1961.

Ullman, E., *Close to the Machine: Technophilia and Its Discontents*, San Francisco, City Lights, 1997.

Walton, K., *Mimesis as Make-Believe*, Cambridge, MA, Harvard University Press, 1990.

Index